Charting the Mesorah: Creation through Geonim

בעזהי״ת

Other volumes in the Hashkafah Library Series

Anvil of Sinai:
An in-depth analysis
of fundamental Torah concepts

Challenge of Sinai:
A Torah approach
to a wide range of contemporary problems

The Ethical Personality:
Clarifying the Torah approach to ethics;
including "Iggeres haRamban,"
and "Iggeres haMussar"
of Rabbe Yisroel Salanter

The Halacha and Beyond:
Clarifying the fiscal-ethical
responsibilities of the Torah Jew,
and the bitachon concept

Legacy of Sinai:
A history of Torah transmission,
with world backgrounds:
From Creation through the
close of the Geonic Era [1-4798]

Masters of the Mesorah: Early Rishonim:
A history of Torah transmission,
with world backgrounds;
Geonic Era through Early Rishonim [900-1300]

Masters of the Mesorah: Later Rishonim:
A history of Torah transmission,
with world backgrounds;
Closing centuries of Rishonim era [1100-1575]

The Torah Ethic:
Clarifying the Torah ethic of
"bein adam la-chavero" —
the interpersonal relationship
between man and his fellow man;
including "Ethical Bequest of the Rambam"

Torah Faith: The Thirteen Principles:
An exposition on the
Thirteen Principles of Torah Faith;
including relevant Holocaust narratives

A project of
Hashkafah Publications
Hashkafah History Series

דור דור ומנהיגיו:

מבריאת העולם
עד סוף תקופת הגאונים

מלמד שהראה הקב״ה למשה
כל מה שהיה ועתיד להיות . . .
דור דור ודורשיו,
דור דור ושופטיו,
דור דור ומנהיגיו.
[במדבר רבה כג, ד]

The Holy One, blessed be He,
Showed Moshe everything that was,
And all that is destined to be . . .
Each generation and its teachers,
Each generation and its judges,
Each generation and its [Torah] leaders.
[Bamidbar Rabbah 23:4]

CHARTING THE MESORAH:

Creation through Geonim

by Rabbi Zechariah Fendel

An original collection of Charts,
with concise descriptive narrative units,
Charting the course of Torah Transmission,
from Creation through Geonic Era [1-4800]
Adapted from **Legacy of Sinai.**

Hashkafah History Series
Hashkafah Publications
New York: 5754/1994

Note: Prior works in the Hashkafah Series include *Haskamos* of Maran haGaon Rav Moshe Feinstein, זצוק״ל and Maran haGaon Rav Chaim Pinchas Scheinberg, שליט״א.

Library of Congress Catalogue Number: 88—080514

ISBN: 1—879061—02—3

For further study concerning the various periods covered in these charts, the reader is referred to **Legacy of Sinai**, which provides a wealth of information, documented by an abundance of source references.

All footnotes in these charts refer to Appendices "A" through "G" in **Legacy of Sinai.**

Manufactured in the United States of America

Table of Contents

Narrative Units
Creation through Geonic Era

Unit	Title	Page
I.	Historical Overview: Creation through Close of Geonic Era	7
II.	Adam haRishon: Handiwork of the Creator	16
III.	The Six Basic Commandments; Decline of Mankind	17
IV.	Noach and the Great Deluge; Two Millennia Desolation	19
V.	Avraham Avinu; Yitzchak Avinu; Yaakov Avinu	21
VI.	Yosef: From Bondage to Royalty; Moshe Rabbeinu	25
VII.	The Ten Plagues; Revelation; Joshua	26
VIII.	Era of the Shoftim	28
IX.	The Prophets of Israel	31
X.	House of David	36
XI.	Kingdom of Ephraim	37
XII.	Babylonian Exile	43
XIII.	Return to Zion; Purim; Anshei Knesses haGedolah	44
XIV.	The Zugos; The Early Tannaim	46
XV.	The Later Tannaim; Redaction of the Mishnah	47
XVI.	Early Babylonian Amoraim; Talmud Yerushalmi	52
XVII.	The Eretz Yisroel Amoraim; The Jewish Calendar	53
XVIII.	Redaction of Talmud Bavli; Rabbanan Savorai	54
XIX.	The Geonic Tekufah	59
XX.	Rav Hai Gaon: Closing Decades of Geonic Tekufah	60

Charts and Tables

Creation through Geonic Era

No.	Title	Page
	Overview: Creation through Geonic Era [1-4798]	7-10
I.	Major Tekufos in Torah Transmission	11
II.	Major Epochs in Jewish History	11
III.	1,000 Years Prophecy: The Early Prophets	12
IV.	1,000 Years Prophecy: The Later Prophets	13
V.	Transmission Process: Tannaitic Era	14
VI.	Transmission Process: Amoraitic Era	15
VII.	Ten Generations: Adam to Noach, 1-2006	18
VIII.	Ten Generations: Shem to Avraham, 1558-2123	20
IX.	Six Generations: Yitzchak to Moshe Rabbeinu	22
X.	Prophecy Before Mattan Torah	23
XI.	From Creation through Birth of Yitzchak	24
XII.	From Yitzchak until Crossing of the Jordan	27
XIII.	Chronological Table of the Judges	29
XIV.	Mishkan and Bais HaMikdash Landmark Dates	30
XV.	The Forty-Eight Prophets of Israel	32-33
XVI.	Mattan Torah through Geonic Era	34
XVII.	Redaction of the Twenty-Four Kisvei Kodesh	35
XVIII.	Tracing Mesorah of the Prophets	38-40
XIX.	Historical Highlights of the Temple Site	41
XX.	Seven Tzaddikim who Encompassed All Generations	42
XXI.	Six Thousand Years of Creation	42
XXII.	First Exile Era: Babylonian Exile	45
XXIII.	From Ezra to Hillel haZaken	48
XXIV.	Five Generations of Tannaim	49-50
XXV.	Roman Emperors During Tannaitic Era	50
XXVI.	The Sanhedrin and the Nesi'im During the Tannaitic Era	51
XXVII.	Amoraim and Rabbanan Savorai	55-56
XXVIII.	Eretz Yisroel Roshei Yeshiva — Amoraitic Era	57
XXIX.	Roshei Yeshiva of Sura: Amoraitic Era	57
XXX.	Roshei Yeshiva of Pumbedisa: Amoraitic Era	58
XXXI.	The Geonic Period, 589-1038 C.E.	61-62
XXXII.	Primary Dates in Jewish History	63
XXXIII.	Daniel's Vision Concerning the Four Kingdoms	64

Historical Overview: 1-4798

The following outline will provide the reader with a panoramic overview of the first 4800 years of the Mesorah process, from Creation through the close of the Geonic Era (1-4798) [1038 C.E.].

Ten Generations — Adam to Noach: 1-1056

Among the few righteous individuals during the first ten generations were Adam, Chanoch, Methuselah and Noach. Adam, who died in 930, saw eight generations of his descendants. Noach was born in 1056.

Ten Generations — Noach to Avraham: 1056-1948.

The righteous individuals during these ten generations were Shem and Ever, and, of course, Avraham Avinu. The *Mabbul* took place in 1656, when Noach was six hundred years old. Noach died in 2006, ten years after the transgression of the *Dor Haflagah* — the generation which had undertaken to build the Tower of Bavel.

Five Hundred Years to Mattan Torah: 1948-2448

Five hundred years before *Mattan Torah*, Avraham Avinu was born [1948]. In the year 2000, he embarked upon his course of Torah dissemination. Yitzchak was born four hundred years before *Mattan Torah* [2048], when Avraham was one hundred years old. In the year 2108 Yaakov was born, and he descended to Egypt 130 years later [2238]. His descendants remained in Egypt for 210 years, until the Exodus in 2448.

One Thousand Years Prophecy: 2448-3448

The ensuing one thousand years comprised the era of prophecy [2448-3448]. From a historical perspective, the era of prophecy may be divided into four primary *tekufos*.

(a) Pre-Temple Era — 480 Years [2448-2928]. Beginning with the leadership of Moshe Rabbeinu, and with *Mattan Torah* at Sinai in 2448, this *tekufah* includes the eras of Joshua, the *Shoftim*, Shmuel haNavi, the Kingdom of Saul, and the emergence of the Kingdom of David.

(b) First Temple Era — 410 Years [2928-3338]. This was the era of the Kings of Judah and of Israel. It was during this era, too, that the towering Prophets, Eliyahu and Elisha, Isaiah and Jeremiah, as well as the many other great Prophets of Israel, stirred the conscience of their people as they reawakened them to an awareness of their magnificent destiny. The Kingdom of Ephraim, which seceded from the Kingdom of Judah in 2964, was led into exile by the King of Assyria in 3205. The First Temple was destroyed in 3338, 410 years after its construction by King Solomon in 2928.

(c) Babylonian Exile — 70 Years [3338-3408]. This was the era of the Prophet, Ezekiel, and of Daniel, Ish Chamudos. Construction of the Second Temple began under Cyrus [3390]. The Purim episode began 3 years later [3393-3407].

(d) Second Temple: The Early Decades — 40 Years [3408-3448]. During this period, the foundations of the Second Temple were established by the last Prophets, Chaggai, Zechariah, and Malachi, as well as by Ezra haSofer and the *Anshei Knesses haGedolah*. When Chaggai, Zechariah, and Malachi died in 3448, the one-thousand-year *tekufah* of prophecy came to an end.

The Second Temple Era — 420 Years: 3408-3828

During the Second Temple Era, which lasted 420 years [3408-3828], the Jewish commonwealth came under the rule of four separate dynasties.

(a) Persian-Median Rule — 52 Years [3390-3442]. The Temple construction, which had been interrupted shortly after the reign of Cyrus, resumed in the year 3408. The Temple was completed four years later [3412], during the reign of Darius II, son of King Ahasuerus.

(b) Greek-Macedonian Rule — 180 Years [3442-3622]. This era included the reign of Alexander the Great, and his successors, the Ptolemaic and Seleucid Dynasties, which vied for control of Eretz Yisroel.

(c) Chashmonean Dynasty — 103 Years [3622-3725]. In the year 3622, the Chashmonean uprising began, and the story of Chanukah took place. Chashmonean Kings ruled for the ensuing 103 years.

(d) Herodian Dynasty —103 Years [3725-3828]. In 3725, Herod, the Idumean, overthrew the Chashmonean Dynasty and usurped the throne. With Roman backing, his descendants ruled — with intermittent and concurrent rule of Roman procurators — until the destruction of the Second Temple in 3828 [68 C.E.].

From the point of view of Torah transmission, this Second Temple Era may be divided into three distinct *tekufos*.

(a) Anshei Knesses haGedolah [ca. 3370-3500]. This era began with Ezra haSofer, and ended with Shimon haTzaddik. Prophecy ended with the death of Malachi (Ezra) [3448].

(b) Zugos [ca. 3500-3768]. After the transitional leadership of Antigonos of Socho, five pairs of *Zugos* spanned this era, which ended with the presidency of Hillel haZaken [3728-3768].

(c) Early Tannaitic Era [ca. 3768-3828]. This was the era of the great Academies of Bais Shammai and Bais Hillel. It ended with the transfer of the *Sanhedrin* from Jerusalem to Yavneh by Rabbon Yochanan ben Zakkai, at the time of the Second *Churban*, in 3828 [68 C.E.].

Eretz Yisroel — Post-Churban Era: 3828-ca.4120 [68-360 C.E.]

During the post-*Churban* era, Torah study flourished intermittently in Eretz Yisroel, for approximately three hundred years [3828-*ca.* 4120]. This era may be divided into two distinct *tekufos* of Torah transmission.

(a) Later Tannaitic Era [3828-3960]. After the *Churban*, the country often reeled under the oppressive decrees of many of the Roman Emperors, with a few brief periods of respite during the reign of certain benevolent Roman rulers, such as Marcus Aurelius Antoninus [161-180 C.E.]. Despite the oppressive rule, however, Torah study flourished under such leaders as Rabbe Yehoshua b. Chananiah, Rabbe Eliezer haGadol, Rabbe Akiva and his colleagues, as well as his disciples, Rabbe Meir, Rabbe Yehudah b. Illai, and Rabbe Shimon b. Yochai. This period also saw the compilation and redaction of the Mishnah under Rabbeinu haKadosh, and the close of the Tannaitic era [ca. 3960] (200 C.E.).

(b). Eretz Yisroel Amoraim [ca. 3960-4120]. The second half of this era saw the emergence of the Eretz Yisroel Amoraim in the great Academy of Rabbe Yochanan in Tiberias, as well as the completion of the *Talmud Yerushalmi* one hundred and fifty years later (*ca.* 4110) [350 C.E.], and the arrangement of the Jewish calendar by Hillel haSheni in 4119 [359 C.E.]

Babylonian Era: 3979-4798 [219-1038 C.E.]

For the most part, the Jewish community of Bavel fared far better than their Eretz Yisroel co-religionists. Under a variety of mostly benevolent Babylonian dynasties and rulers, the Torah community thrived in Bavel from the time of the First *Churban* in 3338, until the close of the Geonic era almost fifteen hundred years later, in 4798. Bavel became a primary Torah center with the descent of Rav to Bavel in 3979, and the Yeshivos of Sura/Masa-Machsya, and Nehardea/Pumbedisa remained the central Torah academies of *Klall Yisroel,* until the death of Rav Hai Gaon more than eight hundred years later, in 4798.

This era, too, may be divided into three distinct *tekufos* of Torah transmission.

(a) Amoraitic Era [3979-4235]. This era saw the compilation and redaction of the Babylonian Talmud by Rav Ashi [d. 4187] and Ravina, as well as the termination of *Hora'ah* with the death of Ravina II, in 4235 [475 C.E.].

(b) Rabbanan Savorai [4235-4350]. This era included the חתימת התלמוד — the final completion of the Babylonian Talmud, in 4260 [500 C.E.].

(c) Geonic Era [4350-4798]. This era, which commenced with the installation of Mar Chanan of Ashkaya as the first Gaon of Pumbedisa in 4349, came to a close with the death of Rav Hai Gaon, in 4798. Some of the great scholars of this era were Rav Yehudai Gaon [*Halachos Pesukos*], Rav Achai of Shabcha [*She'iltos*], Rav Shimon Kayyara [*Halachos Gedolos*], Rav Amram Gaon [*Siddur*], Rav Saadiah Gaon [*Emunos veDe'os*], and Rav Sherira Gaon [*Iggeres Rav Sherira Gaon*]. With the death of his son, Rav Hai Gaon, the era of Torah centralization came to an end, in the year 4798 (1038 C.E.).

Table I
Major Tekufos in Torah Transmission

Tekufah	Dates	Interval
Moshe Rabbeinu	2448-2488	1,000 years prophecy[1]
Yehoshua	2488-2516	
Zekenim - Shoftim[1]	2517-2871	
Nvi'im[2]	2871-3448	
Early Prophets	(2871-3130)	
Latter Prophets	(3130-3448)	
Anshei Knesses haGedolah[3]	(3370-3500)	
Tannaitic Era[4]	3500-3960	460 yrs.
Zugos (incl. Antigonos)	(3500-3768)	268 yrs.
Later Tannaim	(3768-3960)	192 yrs.
Amoraitic Era[5]	3960-4235	275 yrs.
Rabbanan Savorai[5]	4235-4350	125 yrs.
Geonic Era[6]	4350-4798	450 yrs.

(1) See Table XIII   (2) See Table XV   (3) See Table XXIII
(4) See Table XXIV   (5) See Table XXVII   (6) See Table XXXI

Table II
Major Epochs in Jewish History

Era	Dates	Interval
Pre-Temple Era[1]	**2448-2928**	**480 yrs.**
First Temple Era[2]	**2928-3338**	**410 yrs.**
Kingdom of Ephraim[3]	(2964-3205)	240 yrs.
Babylonian Exile[4]	**3338-3408**	**70 yrs.**
Second Temple Era[2]	**3408-3828**	**420 yrs.**
Foreign Rule[5]	(3408-3622)	214 yrs.
Chashmonean Rule[5]	(3622-3725)	103 yrs.
Herodian Dynasty[5]	(3725-3828)	103 yrs.

(1) I K 6:1   (2) Yoma 9a   (3) Ezekiel 4:5,R   (4) Ezra 1:1,R   (5) Av. Zar. 9a

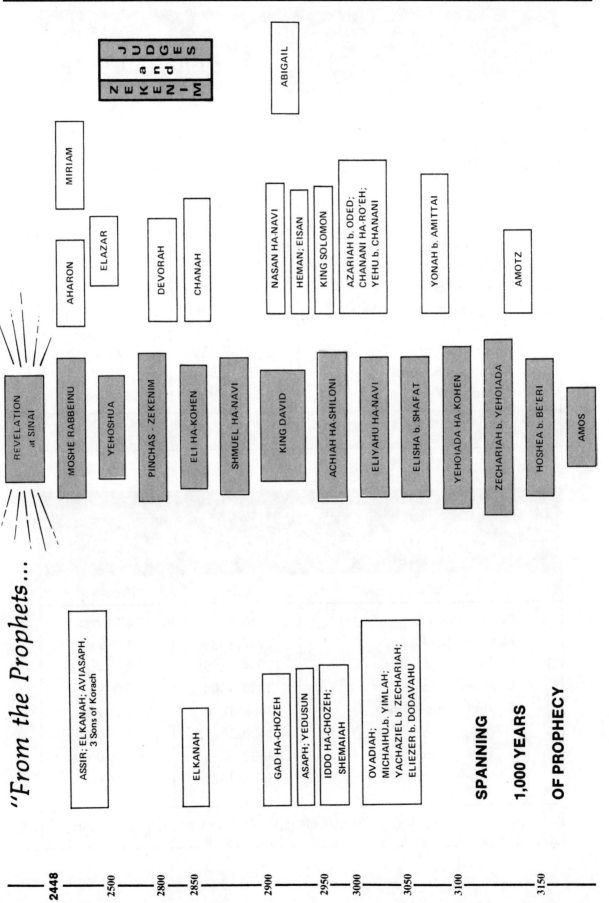

THE EARLY PROPHETS

"From the Prophets..."

SPANNING

1,000 YEARS

OF PROPHECY

	JUDGES
	Kings
	ZEN-IM

REVELATION at SINAI

MOSHE RABBEINU
AHARON
MIRIAM
ASSIR; ELKANAH; AVIASAPH, 3 Sons of Korach

YEHOSHUA
ELAZAR

PINCHAS - ZEKENIM
DEVORAH
ELKANAH

ELI HA-KOHEN
CHANAH

SHMUEL HA-NAVI

KING DAVID
NASAN HA-NAVI
HEMAN; EISAN
KING SOLOMON
GAD HA-CHOZEH
ASAPH; YEDUSUN
IDDO HA-CHOZEH; SHEMAIAH

ACHIAH HA-SHILONI
AZARIAH b. ODED;
CHANANI HA-RO'EH;
YEHU b. CHANANI
OVADIAH;
MICHAIHU.b. YIMLAH;
YACHAZIEL b ZECHARIAH;
ELIEZER b. DODAVAHU

ELIYAHU HA-NAVI

ELISHA b. SHAFAT

YEHOIADA HA KOHEN
YONAH b. AMITTAI

ZECHARIAH b. YEHOIADA

HOSHEA b. BE'ERI
AMOTZ

AMOS

ABIGAIL

2448
2500
2800
2850
2900
2950
3000
3050
3100
3150

12

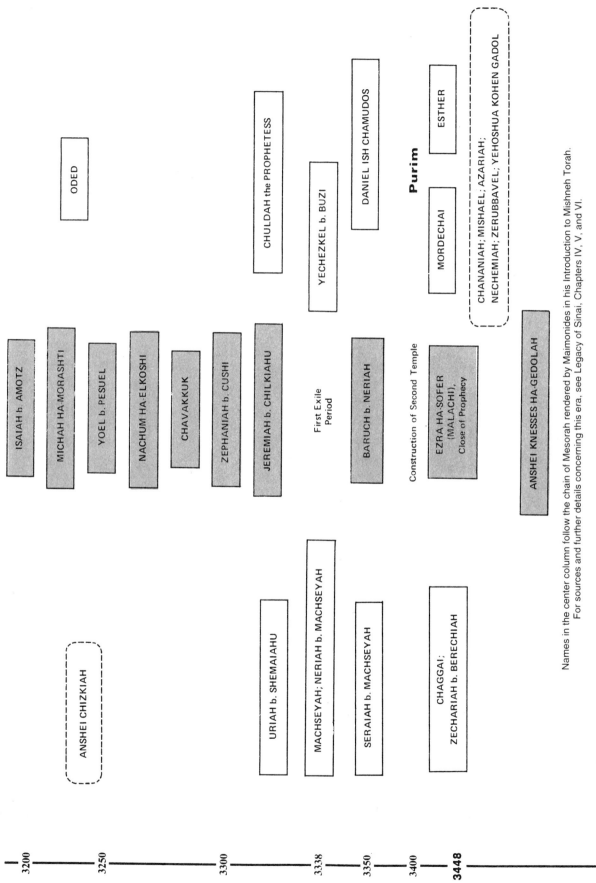

THE LATTER PROPHETS

3200	ISAIAH b. AMOTZ
	ODED
	MICHAH HA-MORASHTI
3250	YOEL b. PESUEL
	NACHUM HA-ELKOSHI
	CHAVAKKUK
	ANSHEI CHIZKIAH
	ZEPHANIAH b. CUSHI
	CHULDAH the PROPHETESS
3300	JEREMIAH b. CHILKIAHU
	URIAH b. SHEMAIAHU
	First Exile Period
3338	YECHEZKEL b. BUZI
	MACHSEYAH; NERIAH b. MACHSEYAH
	BARUCH b. NERIAH
3350	DANIEL ISH CHAMUDOS
	SERAIAH b. MACHSEYAH
	Construction of Second Temple
3400	EZRA HA-SOFER (MALACHI), Close of Prophecy
	CHAGGAI; ZECHARIAH b. BERECHIAH
	Purim
	MORDECHAI ESTHER
3448	CHANANIAH; MISHAEL; AZARIAH; NECHEMIAH; ZERUBBAVEL; YEHOSHUA KOHEN GADOL
	ANSHEI KNESSES HA-GEDOLAH

Names in the center column follow the chain of Mesorah rendered by Maimonides in his Introduction to Mishneh Torah.
For sources and further details concerning this era, see Legacy of Sinai, Chapters IV, V, and VI.

13

Table V

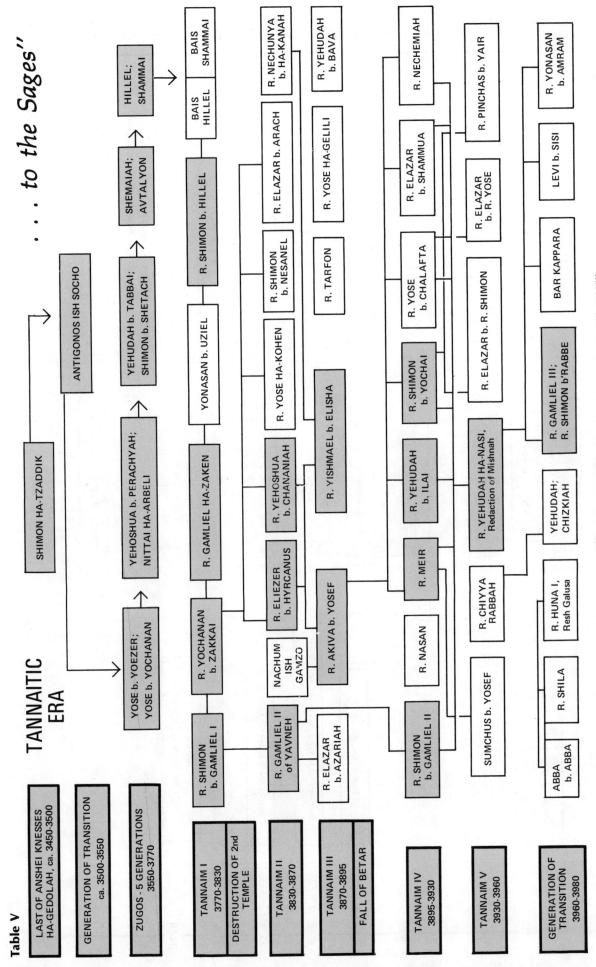

TANNAITIC ERA

. . . . to the Sages"

LAST OF ANSHEI KNESSES
HA-GEDOLAH, ca. 3450-3500

GENERATION OF TRANSITION
ca. 3500-3550

ZUGOS - 5 GENERATIONS
3550-3770

TANNAIM I
3770-3830

DESTRUCTION OF 2nd
TEMPLE

TANNAIM II
3830-3870

TANNAIM III
3870-3895

FALL OF BETAR

TANNAIM IV
3895-3930

TANNAIM V
3930-3960

GENERATION OF
TRANSITION
3960-3980

SHIMON HA-TZADDIK

ANTIGONOS ISH SOCHO

YOSE b. YOEZER;
YOSE b. YOCHANAN

YEHOSHUA b. PERACHYAH;
NITTAI HA-ARBELI

YEHUDAH b. TABBAI;
SHIMON b. SHETACH

SHEMAIAH;
AVTALYON

HILLEL; SHAMMAI

BAIS HILLEL   BAIS SHAMMAI

R. SHIMON b. HILLEL

YONASAN b. UZIEL

R. GAMLIEL HA-ZAKEN

R. YOCHANAN b. ZAKKAI

R. SHIMON b. GAMLIEL

R. GAMLIEL II of YAVNEH

R. ELAZAR b. AZARIAH

R. ELIEZER b. HYRCANUS

NACHUM ISH GAMZO

R. YEHOSHUA b. CHANANIAH

R. YOSE HA-KOHEN

R. ELAZAR b. ARACH

R. NECHUNYA b. HA-KANAH

R. SHIMON b. NESANEL

R. YISHMAEL b. ELISHA

R. TARFON

R. YOSE HA-GELILI

R. YEHUDAH b. BAVA

R. AKIVA b. YOSEF

R. SHIMON b. GAMLIEL II

R. NASAN

R. MEIR

R. YEHUDAH b. ILAI

R. SHIMON b. YOCHAI

R. YOSE b. CHALAFTA

R. ELAZAR b. SHAMMUA

R. NECHEMIAH

SUMCHUS b. YOSEF

R. CHIYYA RABBAH

R. YEHUDAH HA-NASI,
Redaction of Mishnah

R. ELAZAR b. R. SHIMON

R. ELAZAR b. R. YOSE

R. PINCHAS b. YAIR

ABBA b. ABBA

R. SHILA

R. HUNA I, Resh Galusa

YEHUDAH; CHIZKIAH

R. GAMLIEL III; R. SHIMON b'RABBE

BAR KAPPARA

LEVI b. SISI

R. YONASAN b. AMRAM

For sources and further details concerning this era, see **Legacy of Sinai**, Chapters VII and VIII.

14

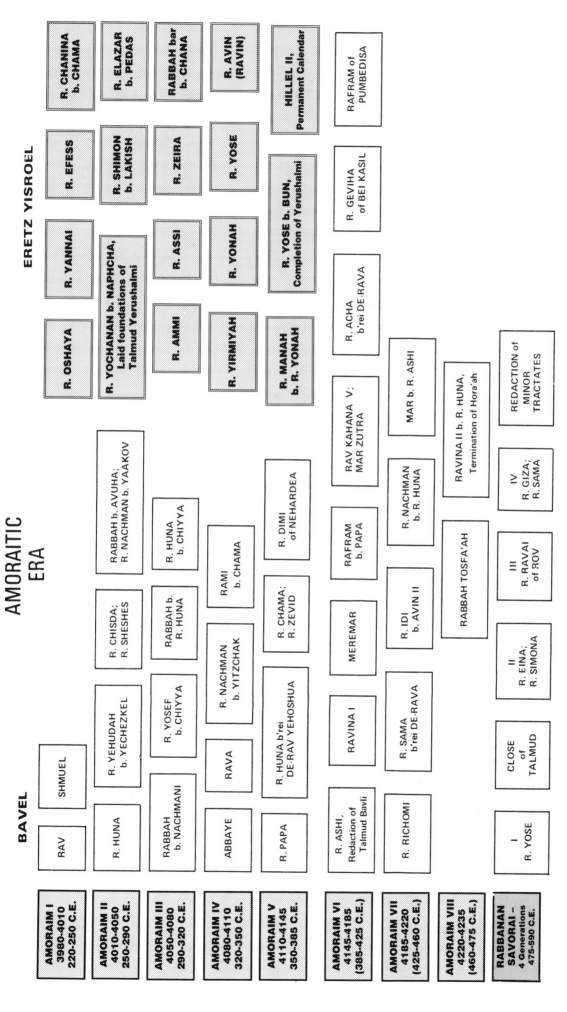

AMORAITIC ERA

BAVEL   **ERETZ YISROEL**

Generation	BAVEL	ERETZ YISROEL
AMORAIM I — 3980-4010 / 220-250 C.E.	RAV; SHMUEL	R. CHANINA b. CHAMA; R. EFESS; R. OSHAYA
AMORAIM II — 4010-4050 / 250-290 C.E.	R. HUNA; R. YEHUDAH b. YECHEZKEL	R. ELAZAR b. PEDAS; R. SHIMON b. LAKISH; R. YANNAI; R. YOCHANAN b. NAPHCHA, Laid foundations of Talmud Yerushalmi
AMORAIM III — 4050-4080 / 290-320 C.E.	RABBAH b. NACHMANI; R. YOSEF b. CHIYYA; R. CHISDA; R. SHESHES; RABBAH b. AVUHA; R. NACHMAN b. YAAKOV	RABBAH bar b. CHANA; R. ZEIRA; R. ASSI; R. AMMI
AMORAIM IV — 4080-4110 / 320-350 C.E.	ABBAYE; RAVA; R. NACHMAN b. YITZCHAK; RABBAH b. R. HUNA; R. HUNA b. CHIYYA	R. AVIN (RAVIN); R. YOSE; R. YONAH; R. YIRMIYAH
AMORAIM V — 4110-4145 / 350-385 C.E.	R. PAPA; R. HUNA b'rei DE-RAV YEHOSHUA; R. CHAMA; R. ZEVID; RAMI b. CHAMA; R. DIMI of NEHARDEA	HILLEL II, Permanent Calendar; R. YOSE b. BUN, Completion of Yerushalmi; R. MANAH b. R. YONAH
AMORAIM VI — 4145-4185 (385-425 C.E.)	R. ASHI, Redaction of Talmud Bavli; RAVINA I; MEREMAR; RAFRAM b. PAPA; RAV KAHANA V; MAR ZUTRA	RAFRAM of PUMBEDISA; R. GEVIHA of BEI KASIL; R. ACHA b'rei DE-RAVA
AMORAIM VII — 4185-4220 (425-460 C.E.)	R. RICHOMI; R. SAMA b'rei DE-RAVA; R. IDI b. AVIN II; R. NACHMAN b. R. HUNA; MAR b. R. ASHI	
AMORAIM VIII — 4220-4235 (460-475 C.E.)	CLOSE of TALMUD; RABBAH TOSFA'AH; RAVINA II b. R. HUNA, Termination of Hora'ah	
RABBANAN SAVORAI – 4 Generations 475-590 C.E.	I R. YOSE; II R. EINA; R. SIMONA; III R. RAVAI of ROV; IV R. GIZA; R. SAMA; REDACTION of MINOR TRACTATES	

Most of the Amoraim cited in this Chart stood at the helm of the great academies of Sura, Masa Machsya, Naresh, Nehardea, Pumbedisa, or Mechoza. For sources and further details concerning this era, see Legacy of Sinai: Chapters IX, X, and XI.

15

ADAM HA-RISHON — HANDIWORK OF THE CREATOR

The starting point of the Jewish calendar is marked by the creation of Adam haRishon on *Erev Shabbos,* 1 Tishrei of the year 1, although the initial process of Creation itself took place five days earlier, on 25 Ellul of the zero year, when the Eternal created the world from אפס המוחלט — from utter nothingness.

On the morning of the sixth day of Creation, the Almighty fashioned Adam out of the earth, on the very site where the מזבח — the sacrificial altar — was destined to stand in the *Bais HaMikdash,* some three millennia later, so that man might be worthy of attaining atonement for his sins. Chava was created that same afternoon, and together they entered *Gan Eden.* On the same day, Cain and Abel were born.

Magnificent Stature of Adam haRishon

The spiritual stature of Adam haRishon — יציר כפיו של הקב״ה — handiwork of the Creator — was so magnificent that it surpassed even that of the *Malachim* themselves. Nevertheless, on the very day of their creation, Adam and Chava succumbed to temptation and to the wiles of the *nachash ha-kadmon* — the wily serpent — and they sinned. In so doing, Adam fell from his lofty stature, dragging down, not only himself, but all of creation with him.

On that very same day, too, they were driven from Gan Eden. When the sun set on Friday evening, Adam thought that the ensuing darkness was a punishment for his transgression, and he bemoaned the fact that he had caused the world to be engulfed in darkness. When the sun rose again on Shabbos morning, he rejoiced. Whereupon, Adam erected a *mizbe'ach* on the site of the Temple altar, and brought a thanksgiving offering to G-d.

The Mizbe'ach

It was on this very same site that Cain and Abel later brought their offerings to G-d. It was here that Noach brought his offering when he emerged from the Ark, and it was here, too, that the *Akedas Yitzchak* later took place. This was also the site of King David's *mizbe'ach* in Goren Arnon, as well as the site of the *mizbe'ach* in both the First Temple and the Second Temple.

As Adam brought his thanksgiving offering, he joyously recited the ninety-second psalm — מזמור שיר ליום השבת — *"A Psalm of song for the Sabbath Day."*

THE SIX BASIC COMMANDMENTS

After his transgression, Adam was given the following six commandments by the Almighty. He was instructed to refrain from (a) idolatry (b) adultery and incest (c) murder (d) stealing (e) "blessing" the exalted Name of the Creator, and (f) he was instructed to establish a system of law and order, and to adminster justice.

Adam lived 930 years, and he saw eight generations of his descendants. According to a tradition of the Sages, the Almighty showed Adam prophetically דור דור ודורשיו — "all future generations and their leaders."

The Decline of Mankind

It was not very long, however, before mankind strayed from its fulfillment of the six basic commandments. Murder and fratricide commenced when Cain slew Abel. Subsequently, Cain repented for his grave transgression. It was Cain who taught mankind about the far-reaching significance of repentance, without which the world could not possibly continue to exist.

Idolatry was introduced during the generation of Adam's grandson, Enosh (b. 235). As punishment for this iniquity, a huge tidal wave rose from the ocean, and engulfed one-third of the civilized world. With the passing of the generations, the earth was filled with idolatry, immorality, adultery, violence, stealing, corruption, and injustice.

To be sure, during the ten generations between Adam and Noach, there were some exceedingly righteous individuals. According to one interpretation, Chanoch was *"taken by G-d"* in the year 987, to become a *Malach*, because of his righteousness. His son, Methuselah, was also a great *tzaddik*. When he died on 10 Marcheshvon 1656, the *Mabbul* was postponed for seven days in his honor, so that he might be eulogized and mourned for properly.

These individuals, however, could do little to stem the floodtide of iniquity which had engulfed all of mankind.

> *And the L-rd said: I will blot out the man whom I have created from the face of the earth. . . .*
>
> *But Noach found grace in the eyes of the L-rd* [Genesis 6:7-8].

Table VII:

Ten Generations — Adam to Noach, 1-2006*

[Comprising 26 Generations — Creation to Mattan Torah]**

	1	100	200	300	400	500	600	700	800	900	1000	1100	1200	1300	1400	1500	1600	1700	1800	1900	2000

Name	Years
CREATION	1
ADAM	1- 930
SHES	130-1042
ENOSH	235-1140
KEINAN	325-1235
MAHALALEL	395-1290
YERED	460-1422
CHANOCH	622- 987
METHUSELAH	687-1656
LEMECH	874-1651
NOACH	1056-2006

*According to Avos 5:2.   **See Bereshis Rabbah 1:5; Cf. Shabbos 88b, Rashi, s.v. 974 Doros.

18

NOACH AND THE GREAT DELUGE

In the tenth generation, Noach was born in 1056 — one *tzaddik* in an evil world. 120 years prior to the *Mabbul*, in the year 1536, the Almighty pronounced His final judgment upon all living things, providing mankind with ample opportunity for repentance.

On the seventeenth day of Marcheshvon, 1656, the flood waters of the *Mabbul* brought annihilation upon all living things. The judgment of the *Dor haMabbul* lasted one complete solar year.

A New World

When Noach emerged from the ark, he erected a *mizbe'ach,* and offered up upon it a thanksgiving offering. Like the *mizbe'ach* of Adam haRishon, the *mizbe'ach* of Noach, too, was erected on the site of the *mizbe'ach* which was destined to stand in the Bais HaMikdash.

In addition to the six basic commandments of Adam haRishon, Noach and his descendants were also instructed concerning the prohibition of אבר מן החי — eating a limb cut off from a living animal — thereby together comprising the שבע מצות בני נח — the Seven Noahide Laws. Noach died in the year 2006, four hundred years after the *Mabbul* and ten years after the generation of the *Haflagah* — the dispersal of the nations.

From Noach and his three sons, Shem, Cham, and Yefes, the world was rebuilt anew. Both Shem, and his great-grandson, Ever, were great *tzaddikim,* as well as prophets.

The seven Prohets from Creation until the Egyptian period were: (1) Adam (2) Noach (3) Shem (4) Ever, and the *Avos* (5) Avraham (6) Yitzchak and (7) Yaakov.

שני אלפים תהו — Two Millennia Desolation

Despite the positive influence of Noach, his son, Shem, and his great-grandson, Ever, the descendants of Noach, too, sinned grievously. In 1996, they began building the great Tower of Bavel, in an attempt to do battle with the Almighty. Whereupon, they were divided into many tongues, and were scattered over the face of the earth.

Noach died ten years later, in the year 2006.

The first two thousand years since Creation were referred to as שני אלפים תהו — "Two Millennia of Spiritual Desolation."

Table VIII: Ten Generations — Shem to Avraham, 1558-2123*

[Comprising 26 Generations — Creation to Mattan Torah]**

	1000	1100	1200	1300	1400	1500	1600	1700	1800	1900	2000	2100	2200

[NOACH]	1056-2006
SHEM	1558-2158
MABBUL	1656
ARPACHSHAD	1658-2096
SHELACH	1693-2126
EVER	1723-2187
PELEG	1757-1996
HAFLAGAH	1996
RE'U	1787-2026
SERUG	1819-2049
NACHOR	1849-1997
TERACH	1878-2083
AVRAHAM	1948-2123

*According to Avos 5:2.   **See Bereshis Rabbah 1:5; Cf. Shabbos 88b, Rashi, s.v. 974 Doros.

AVRAHAM AVINU — BELOVED OF G-D

In Nisan 1948, 500 years before *Mattan Torah*, Avraham Avinu was born. He recognized the Creator at an early age. In the year 2,000, when he was fifty-two years old, Avraham embarked on his life's goal of bringing all mankind to a recognition of G-d. This marked the beginning of שני אלפים תורה — "Two Millennia of Torah" — which came to a close some fifty years after the redaction of the Mishnah by Rabbeinu haKadosh, in 3948 (188 C.E.) — 500 years after the close of Prophecy.

The Almighty tested Avraham's faith with ten exceedingly severe trials. When Avraham successfully withstood each of these tests — including the trial of the *Akedah* — an eternal covenant of love was forged between G-d and Avraham.

YITZCHAK AVINU AND THE MAGNIFICENT AKEDAH

Avraham transmitted his monotheistic life-ideal to his son, Yitzchak, who was born on 15 Nisan, 2048, precisely 400 years before the Exodus, in fulfillment of G-d's promise that *"your children shall be sojourners in a land that is not their own . . . for 400 years."* [Genesis 5:13]

In the year 2085, the magnificent event of the *Akedah* took place on Mt. Moriah, at the site where the Temple would later be built. In the same year, Sarah died, and Rivkah was born.

YAAKOV AVINU — "THE CHOSEN OF THE PATRIARCHS"

When Yitzchak was sixty years old [2108], Yaakov Avinu — the בחיר שבאבות — the "chosen of the Patriarchs" — was born. He was "a dweller of tents." He studied Torah in the Yeshiva of Ever, as well as in the Yeshiva of Avraham Avinu.

Rachel and Leah, who were twins, were born on the day that Yitzchak blessed Yaakov, in 2171.

Eleven of Yaakov's sons were born at seven-month intervals in the house of Lavan [2193-2199]. Binyamin was born 8 years after his brother, Yosef [2207], when Yaakov was traveling home, at which time his mother, Rachel, died. She was buried on the road to Bais Lechem, which, to this very day, is one of Israel's holiest sites. Rivkah died in the same year. Leah died nine years later [2216], and was buried in the Me'oras haMachpelah, in Chevron, where all the *Avos* and *Imahos* were buried, as well as Adam and Chava.

Table IX: Six Generations — Yitzchak to Moshe Rabbeinu, 2048-2488*

Comprising 26 Generations — Creation to Mattan Torah*

1900 1950 2000 2050 2100 2150 2200 2250 2300 2350 2400 2450 2500

[AVRAHAM]	1948-2123
SARAH	1958-2085
TORAH DISSEMINATION	2000
YITZCHAK	2048-2228
RIVKAH	2085-2207
YAAKOV	2108-2255
RACHEL	2171-2207
LEAH	2171-2216
LEVI	2194-2331
KEHOS	2225-2358**
AMRAM	2250-2387**
YOCHEVED	2238-2489**
MOSHE	2368-2488

MATTAN TORAH 6 Sivan, 2448

* See Bereshis Rabbah 1:5; Cf. Shabbos 88b, Rashi, s.v. 974 Doros.

** Dates of Kehos and Amram are approximated, following Exodus 6:18; 6:20; and Rashbam, Bava Basra 121b. Re. Yocheved, see Seder Olam, Chapter 9, G'ra, nn. 5, 6; Bava Basra 120a. All other dates are precise and are based on sources as rendered in Tables XI and XII, and in Appendix "A," in Legacy of Sinai.

22

Table X

Prophecy before Mattan Torah*

7 Prophets, Pre-Egyptian Era**

Name	Date	Source
Adam	1- 930	Gen. 2:16
Noach	1056-2006	Gen. 6:9,13
Shem	1558-2158	Gen 25:23,R
Ever	1723-2187	Gen. 10:25,R
Avraham	1948-2123	Gen. 20:7
Yitzchak	2048-2228	Gen. 26:2
Yaakov	2108-2255	Gen. 31:3,R

The Imahos [Matriarchs]***

Name	Date	Source
Sarah	1958-2085	Gen. 11:29,R; Gen. 21:12,R
Rivkah	2085-2207	Gen. 27:42,R; Beresh. Rab. 67
Rachel	2171-2207	T. Yerushalmi Ber. 9:3 (66b)
Leah	2171-2216	Gen. 3:21,R; Tanch., ad. loc.

Seven Prophets in Egypt

Name	Date	Source
Moshe	2368-2488	Deut. 34:10
Aharon	2365-2487	Levit. 10:8
Zimri		
Eisan		
Heiman	5 grandsons of Yehudah ben Yaakov Avinu	I Kings 5:11; I Chronicles 2:6
Chalkol		
Darda		

Seven Non-Jewish Prophets****

Name	Source
Balaam	Num. 23:4
Be'or (his father)	B.B. 15b
Job	Job 1:1; Job 38:1
Eliphaz	Job 4:1
Bildad	Job 8:1
Tzofar	Job 11:1
Elihu b. Berachel	Job 32:11

Seven Prophetesses of Israel

Name	Date	Source
Sarah	1958-2085	Gen. 11:29,R
Miriam	2361-2487	Exodus 15:20
Devorah	fl. 2636-2676	Judges 4:4
Chanah	fl. c. 2871	I S 2:1
Abigail	fl. c. 2884	Megillah 14b
Chuldah	fl. 3285-3316	II K 22:14
Esther	fl. 3393-3407	Esther 9:29

* This Table is based upon Seder Olam Rabbah, Chapters 20 and 21, as emended by the Vilna Gaon.

** See Appendix "C," n. 1(A).   *** See Appendix "C," n. 1(B), in "Legacy of Sinai."

**** After Mattan Torah, prophecy among non-Jews ceased entirely (see Rashi, Exodus 33:16-17).

Legend: B.B. = Bava Basra; Ber. = Berachos; Beresh. Rab. = Bereshis Rabbah; Deut. = Deuteronomy; fl. = flourished; Gen. = Genesis; K = Kings; Levit. = Leviticus; Num. = Numbers; R = Rashi; S = Samuel; T = Talmud; Tan. = (Midrash) Tanchuma.

Table XI - Major Events: 1-2048
From Creation through Birth of Yitzchak

Chronological Events	Age of Father at Son's Birth	Date From Creation	Source
Creation[1]			Gen. 1:1
Adam		1	Gen. 1:27
Shes	130	130	Gen. 5:3
Enosh	105	235	Gen. 5:6
Idolatry begins[2]			Gen. 4:26, R
Keinan	90	325	Gen. 5:9
Mahalalel	70	395	Gen. 5:12
Yered	65	460	Gen. 5:15
Chanoch	162	622	Gen. 5:18
Methuselah	65	687	Gen. 5:21
Lemech	187	874	Gen. 5:25
Adam d.		930	Gen. 5:5
Noah	182	1056	Gen. 5:28
Shem[3]	502	1558	Gen. 5:32
Methuselah d.[4]		1656	Gen. 5:27
The Mabbul		1656	Gen. 7:6, 11
Arpachshad	100	1658	Gen. 11:10
Shelach	35	1693	Gen. 11:12
Ever	30	1723	Gen. 11:14
Peleg	34	1757	Gen. 11:16
Re'u	30	1787	Gen. 11:18
Serug	32	1819	Gen. 11:20
Nachor	30	1849	Gen. 11:22
Terach	29	1878	Gen. 11:24
Avraham Avinu	70	1948	Gen. 11:26
Birth of Sarah		1958	Gen. 17:17
Dor Haflagah[5]		1996	S.O. 1
Torah dissemination[6]		2000	S.O. 1
"Two Millenia Torah" begin[6]		2000	Av. Zar. 9a
Death of Noah		2006	Gen. 2:29
"Bris bein haBesarim"[7]		2018	S.O.1
Birth of Yishmael		2034	Gen. 16:16
Avraham circumcised		2047	Gen. 17:24
Sodom destroyed		2047	Gen. 18:16
Birth of Yitzchak		2048	Gen. 21:5

Individuals whose names are rendered in bold on Table XI were Prophets (See S.O. 21).

Legend: **Av. Zar.**= Avodah Zarah; **Ex.**= Exodus; **Gen.**= Genesis;
Pesik. Rab.= Pesikta Rabbah; **R**= Rashi; **S.O.**= Seder Olam.

For Explanatory Notes concerning Table XI, see Appendix "A," in "Legacy of Sinai"

YOSEF HA-TZADDIK — FROM BONDAGE TO ROYALTY

Yosef was abducted from his father's home in 2216, when he was seventeen years old. At the age of thirty [2229], he stood before Pharaoh and became Viceroy of Egypt. Nine years later, upon conclusion of the second year of the famine [2238], Yaakov and his sons descended into Egypt, and the first Exile of Israel began. Two hundred and ten years later [2448], they were redeemed.

Throughout his years of bondage and of royalty, Yosef remained steadfast in his righteousness and unswerving in his faith. Yosef haTzaddik — the perfectly righteous one among his brothers, the *Shivtei Kah* — the perfectly righteous Tribes of G-d — paved the way for Israel in exile, throughout all future generations.

In the Crucible of Egypt

Upon his descent into Egypt, Yaakov sent Yehudah before him to establish a Yeshiva in Goshen, for the Yeshiva has always been the life-line of Israel.

When Yaakov died in 2255, at the age of 147, his sons carried his *aron* to Eretz Yisroel, precisely in the same order in which the Israelites would later surround the Holy Ark in the wilderness.

The Egyptian bondage did not begin before Levi, the last of the *Shevatim,* died in 2332. It lasted for at least eighty-three years, or almost a full century, for Miriam, who was born in 2361 was named for the מרירות, or the bitterness, of the Egyptian bondage.

MOSHE RABBEINU: STIRRINGS OF REDEMPTION

Yocheved, mother of Moshe and Aharon, was born as the Israelites entered the walls of Egypt [2238]. Aharon was born in 2365, and Moshe was born three years later in 2368, when his mother, Yocheved, was 130 years old. Moshe was 80 years old when he first appeared before Pharaoh as the redeemer of *Klall Yisroel.* Joshua, faithful disciple of Moshe, was born in 2406.

On the ninth of Nisan, 2447, G-d appeared to Moshe in the "Burning Bush." Seven days later — 15 Nisan — Moshe consented to become the redeemer of Israel — and the great Redemption was under way.

THE TEN PLAGUES

The judgment of the Egyptians — the Ten Plagues — lasted one full year. Precisely at midnight, 15 Nisan, 2448, G-d smote the Egyptian first-born, and He led the Israelites out of Egypt. Seven days later, the Israelites crossed the Red Sea, amidst a host of miracles. Whereupon, they sang the beautiful Song of the Sea.

The Magnificent Event of Revelation

In the third month, on Shabbos, 6 Sivan, 2448, the magnificent event of Revelation took place. The world stood still when the Eternal revealed Himself in awesome majestic splendor at Sinai. *Klall Yisroel* was forged into a unique Torah entity.

Forty Years of Miracles

During their forty years in the wilderness, *Klall Yisroel* was surrounded and sustained by an endless array of miracles — clouds of Glory overhead, a pillar of cloud to guide them by day and a pillar of fire by night, manna and quail from Heaven, a rolling well of water — perpetual manifestations of the loving guidance of Divine Providence. Moreover, the Mishkan — the Desert Tabernacle — brought the Divine Presence to descend upon Israel

Moshe Rabbeinu, Master of all Prophets, died on Adar 7, 2488, at the age of 120, at which time he bestowed his farewell blessing upon Israel.

JOSHUA — REFLECTING THE RADIANCE OF MOSHE

On 10 Nisan, 2488, Joshua, devoted disciple of Moshe Rabbeinu — led Israel across the Jordan.

The Sages observe that the countenance of Moshe was like the radiance of the sun, while that of Joshua was like the radiance of the moon, for Joshua reflected the brilliant Torah radiance of Moshe Rabbeinu.

In addition to the seven initial years of conquest and the seven years of division of the land, Joshua led Israel for another fourteen years — twenty-eight years in all [2488-2516]. Joshua died in 2516, at the age of 110.

Table XII - Major Events: 2048 - 2488
From Birth of Yitzchak through Crossing the Jordan

Significant Events	Date	Source
Birth of Yizchok	2048	Gen. 21:5
Akeidah; Sarah d.; Rivkah b.[8]	2085	S.O.1
Birth of Yaakov	2108	Gen. 25:26
Death of Avraham	2123	Gen. 25:7
Death of Shem b. Noah	2158	Gen. 11:11
Jacob blessed; Leah, Rachel b[9 10]	2171	S.O.2
Yaakov weds Leah, Rachel[11]	2192	S.O.2
Eleven Shevatim born[12]	2193-99	Ibid.
Birth of Levi	2194	Ibid.
Birth of Yosef	2199	Ibid.
Binyamin b.; Rivkah, Rachel d. [13]	2207	Ibid.
Leah d.; Yosef sold[14]	2216	Ibid.
Death of Yitzchak	2228	Gen. 35:28
Yosef appointed Viceroy	2229	Gen. 41:46
Yaakov descends to Egypt	2238	Gen. 47:9
Birth of Yocheved[15]	2238	Bava Basra 120a
Death of Yaakov	2255	Gen. 47:28
Death of Yosef	2309	Gen. 50:26
Death of Levi	2331	Ex. 6:16, R
Egyptian bondage begins[16]	2332-61	S.O.3
Birth of Miriam[17]	2361	Ibid.
Birth of Aharon	2365	Ex. 7:7
Birth of Moshe[15]	2368	Ex. 2:1, R
Exodus from Egypt	15 Nisan 2448	Ex. 12:40, R
Manna begins to descend	16 Iyar 2448	Ex. 16:1, R
Mattan Torah[18]	6 Sivan 2448	S.O. 5
First Tablets broken[19]	17 Tammuz 2448	Ta'anis 26a
Complete atonement	Yom Kippur 2449	S.O. 6
Mishkan construction begun	11 Tishrei 2449	Ibid., G'ra, n.5
Completion of Mishkan[20]	25 Kislev 2449	Pesik. Rab. 6:5
Erection of Mishkan	1 Nisan 2449	S.O.7
Meraglim return[21]	9 Av 2449	S.O.8
Miriam d.; Rolling well ceases[22]	10 Nisan 2487	S.O. 9-10
Aharon d.; Annanei Kavod cease	1 Av 2487	Numbers 33:38
Moshe Dies; Manna discontinued[23]	7 Adar 2488	S.O. 10
Israelites cross Jordan	10 Nisan 2488	Joshua 4:19
Remaining manna consumed[24]	16 Nisan 2488	S.O. 10

For Explanatory Notes concerning Table XII, see Appendix "A", in "Legacy of Sinai."

THE ERA OF THE SHOFTIM

Many of the *Shoftim* — the Judges who succeeded Joshua — were outstanding Torah scholars, who stood at the head of the *Sanhedrin* of their generation. The following is the succession of the eighteen *Shoftim* and leaders of Israel, from Joshua [2488-2516] through the era of King David [2884-2924].

(1) Joshua bin Nun (2) Osniel b. Kenaz (3) Ehud b. Gera (4) Shamgar b. Anas (5) Devorah and Barak b. Avinoam (6) Gideon [Yerubaal] (7) Avimelech b. Gideon (8) Tolah b. Puah (9) Yair haGileadi (10) Yiphtach haGileadi (11) Ivtzan [Boaz] (12) Elon haZevuloni (13) Avdon b. Hillel (14) Samson (15) Eli (16) Samuel (17) King Saul (18) King David

Osniel b. Kenaz [2516-2556], a half-brother of Calev ben Yephunneh, was the first of the *Shoftim*. When hundreds of halachos were forgotten during the period of mourning for Moshe Rabbeinu, Osniel retrieved them with his profound Torah wisdom.

Devorah [2636-2676], who was the only woman among the *Shoftim*, was one of the seven Prophetesses of Israel. She accompanied Baruch b. Avinoam when he set out to defeat the armies of Sisera. The Sages have great praise for both Devorah and Chana, mother of Shmuel, for their beautiful songs of thanksgiving to the Almighty for His remarkable help and deliverance.

Ivtzan [2792-2797] was Boaz, of the story of Ruth. **Ruth,** a descendant of Balak b. Tzipor and a daughter of Eglon, King of Moab, rejected her birthright as a Moabite princess, to cling, instead, with intense devotion, to G-d and Torah, and to become a true proselyte and a proud mother in Israel. The great-grandson of Boaz and Ruth was King David.

Samson [2813-2832], is referred to by *Chazal* as one of the lesser *Shoftim*. Nevertheless, he attained *Ru'ach haKodesh* — a step below prophecy. **Avimelech** was not a true *Shofet*. He usurped this post through violence.

Eli, the *Kohen Gadol* [2832-2871], teacher of Shmuel haNavi, represented the generation of transition between the eras of the *Shoftim* and the *Nvi'im*.

Shmuel haNavi was a Prophet of towering stature [2871-2881], who ushered in the era of the *Nvi'im*. Shmuel annointed, first King Saul [2882-2924], and then King David [2884-2894], as Kings of Israel.

Table XIII
Chronological Table of the Judges, 2488-2964

Chronological Events	Yrs. of Rule		Date	Source
Yehoshua b. Nun[1]	28		2488-2516	S.O.12
Israelites enter E.Y.			10 Nisan 2488	Josh. 4:19
7 yrs. conquest			2488-2495	S.O. 11
7 yrs. apportionment			2496-2502	S.O. 11
Shemittah cycle begins[2]			2503	Erach. 12b
Osniel b. Kenaz[3]	40		2516-2556	Judg. 3:11
Ehud b. Gera[3]	80		2556-2636	Judge. 3:30
Shamgar b. Anas[4]	(1/2)		2636-2636	Judg. 3:31
Devorah and Barak[3]	40		2636-2676	Judg. 5:31
Midianite Rule	7		2676-2683	Judg. 6:1
Gideon (Yeruba'al)[5]	40		2683-2723	Judg. 8:28
Avimelech b. Gideon[6]	3		2723-2726	Judg. 9:22
Tola b. Pu'ah	23		2726-2749	Judg. 10:2
Yair haGileadi[7]	22	(-1)	2749-2770	Judg. 10:3
Ammon-Philistine Rule[8]	18		2770-2788	Judg. 10:8
Jews 300 yrs. in E.Y.			2488-2788	Judg. 11:26
Yiphtach haGileadi[9]	6	(-2)	2788-2792	Judg. 12:7
Ivtzan (Boaz)[10]	7	(-2)	2792-2797	Judg. 12:9
Elon haZevuloni[11]	10	(-1)	2797-2806	Judg. 12:11
Avdon b. Hillel[11]	8	(-1)	2806-2813	Judg. 12:14
Samson[11]	20	(-1)	2813-2832	Judg. 15:20
Eli[11][12]	40	(-1)	2832-2871	1 Sam. 4:18
Era of Nvi'im begins[13]				
Samuel[14]	10		2871-2881	S.O. 13
Samuel and Saul[14]	1		2881-2882	S.O. 13
Saul[14]	2		2882-2884	S.O. 13
Death of Samuel[15]			2884	S.O. 13
David[16]	40		2884-2924	II S 5:4-5
Solomon (until construction of First Temple)[17]	4		2924-2928	I K 6:1, 37
480 yrs. from Exodus			2448-2928	I K 6:1
Solomon's entire reign	40		2924-2964	I K 11:42

Prophets during this era were: Yehoshua, Pinchas, Devorah, Elkanah, and Chanah (parents of Shmuel), Eli, Shmuel, David, Gad, Nasan, Solomon, and Abigail (wife of David). (S.O. 21; See Appendix "B," n. 1; Appendix "C," n. 1, in "Legacy of Sinai.")

See Appendix "B" for Explanatory Notes concerning this table.
See Table XIV for Mishkan and Bais HaMikdash Landmark Dates.

Legend: Erach. = Erachin; **E.Y.** = Eretz Yisroel; **Judg.** = Judges; **K** = Kings; **S** = Samuel; **S.O.** = Seder Olam.

Table XIV
Mishkan and Bais HaMikdash Landmark Dates

Tekufah	Dates	Duration	Source
Erection of Mishkan	2449-2449	1/2 yrs.	Tan. 29a; Zev. 118b
Desert	2449-2488	39 yrs.	Tan. 29a; Zev. 118b
Gilgal	2488-2502	14 yrs.	S.O. 11; Zev. 118b*
Shiloh	2502-2871	369 yrs.	S.O. 11; Zev. 118b
Nov	2871-2884	13 yrs.	S.O. 13; Zev. 118b
Givon	2884-2928	44 yrs.	S.O. 14; Zev. 118b
480 years from Exodus			1 Kings 6:1
First Temple Era	2928-3338	410 yrs.	Yoma 9a; Haggai 2:9,R; Yad. Hil. Shemittah 10:3
Babylonian Exile	3338-3408	70 yrs.	Dan. 9:2 Ezra 1:2,R**
Second Temple Era	3408-3828	420 yrs.	Yoma 9a; Hag. 2:9,R; Erachin 12b; B.B. 30,R

*See Appendix "B," n. 12, in "Legacy of Sinai."   ** See Appendix "D," n. 14.

Legend: B.B. = Bava Basra; Dan. = Daniel; Hag = Haggai; Hil. = Hilchos; K = Kings; R = Rashi; S.O. = Seder Olam; Tan. = Ta'anis; Yad = Mishneh Torah; Zev. = Zevachim

THE MISHKAN AND THE BAIS HA-MIKDASH

The Mikdash, or the Sanctuary, was always the spiritual heart of the Jewish People. It was instrumental in bringing the *Shechinah* — the Divine Presence — to dwell among the People of Israel. ועשו לי מקדש, ושכנתי בתוכם — *They shall build unto Me a Sanctuary, that I might dwell among them.* [Exodus 25:8]

In the desert, the Jewish People built the Mishkan — the traveling Sanctuary. They carried the Mishkan across the Jordan when they entered the Holy Land. The Mishkan stood, first in Gilgal [14 years], then in Shiloh [369 years], Nov [13 years], and Givon [44 years], for a total of 480 years from the Exodus.

In 2928 King Solomon built the Temple on Mt. Moriah in Jerusalem. The First Temple stood 410 years [2928-3338]. The Second Temple, which was built after the 70-year Babylonian Exile, stood 420 years [3408-3828].

Upon its destruction in 3828, only the *Kosel Ma'aravi* — the Western Wall which surrounded the Temple Mount, remained standing. "The presence of the *Shechinah*," the Sages observe, "has never been removed from the Western Wall."

THE PROPHETS OF ISRAEL

Beginning with Shmuel haNavi [2871-2881] the *tekufah* of the *Nvi'im* extended for well over five hundred years, until the close of prophecy with the deaths of Chaggai, Zechariah and Malachi [3442], thirty-four years after the construction of the Second Temple, in 3408. According to some, prophecy terminated in 3448, precisely one thousand years after *Mattan Torah.*

Maimonides cites the names of the following illustrious Torah personalities as the primary line of succession of the transmission of the Oral Law from Moshe Rabbeinu through the close of the *tekufah* of the Prophets.

(1) Moshe Rabbeinu (2) Joshua (3) Pinchas and Zekenim (4) Eli (5) Samuel (6) David (7) Achiah haShiloni (8) Eliyahu (9) Elisha (10) Yehoiada haKohen (11) Zechariah b. Yehoiada (12) Hoshea (13) Amos (14) Isaiah (15) Michah (16) Yoel (17) Nachum (18) Chavakuk (19) Zephaniah (20) Jeremiah (21) Baruch b. Neriah (22) Ezra haSofer.

While well over a million Jews attained the high level of prophetic revelation during the 1000-year era of Prophecy [2448-3448], only those prophecies which were of significance to later generations were transcribed. The names of the many other Prophets were therefore not included among the forty-eight primary Prophets and seven Prophetesses of Israel.

Fearless Chastisement

Among the towering Prophets of the First Temple era were Achiah haShiloni, Eliyahu haNavi, and Elisha. Isaiah was known as the Prophet of consolation; Jeremiah, as the Prophet of *churban.*

At great peril to themselves, the Prophets chastised Israel incessantly. More than one Prophet was persecuted by the recalcitrant rulers. Hundreds of Prophets were put to death by Jezebel, wife of King Achav. Zechariah b. Yehoiada was slain at the command of Yehoash. The Prophet Isaiah was put to death by Menasheh. Jeremiah was cast into the dungeon time and again by Yehoiakim and Tzidkiahu, at times perilously approaching death. Nevertheless, the Prophets did not desist in their call to repentance. But their prophecies went unheeded, and on the ninth of Av, 3338, the magnificent Temple, which had been erected by Solomon 410 years earlier [2928], went up in flames.

Table XV:
The 48 Prophets of Israel, 2448-3448*

Name	Date	Source
[Avraham]**	1948-2123	Genesis 20:7
[Yitzchak]**	2048-2228	Genesis 26:2
[Yaakov]**	2108-2255	Genesis 21:3, R
Revelation at Sinai	6 Sivan, 2448	SO 5, G'ra, n. 16
(Moshe Rabbeinu)	2368-2488	Ex. 2:1, R; SO 10
[Aharon]**	2365-2487	Numbers 11:6
1. **Joshua**	2406-2516	SO, beg. Ch. 12
2. Assir	fl. c. 2488	Ex. 6:24;
3. Elkanah	fl. c. 2488	Psalm 44:1; 45:1;
4. Aviasaph	fl. c. 2488	46:1; 47:1; 48:1
5. **Pinchas and Zekenim**	2516-2832	Judg. 6:8,R; I S 1:1 ,R
[Eli haKohen]1(E)**	2832-2871	I S 4:18
6. Elkanah	fl. c. 2850	I S 2:27, R
7. **Shmuel haRamassi**	2871-2884	I S 3:4; SO 13, G'ra, n.1
8. **King David**1a	2884-2924	II S 5:4-5
9. Gad haChozeh	fl. c. 2883	I S 22:5, II S 24:11
10. Asaph1b		Psalms 50:1; 73:1
11. Yedusun1b		Psalms 39:1, 62:1
12. Heiman1b	c. 2884-2924 I C 25:1, R	Psalms 88:1
13. Eisan1b		Psalms 89:1
14. Nasan haNavi 1c	fl. c. 2910-2924	II S 7:2; I K 1:11
15. **Achiah haShiloni**3	fl. c. 2924-2960	I K 6:11, Radak; 11:29
[King Solomon]1a**	2924-2964	I K II:42
16. Shemaiah	fl. c. 2964	I K 12:22
17. Iddo haChozeh	fl. c. 2970	I K 13:1, R; II C 9:29
18. Azariah b. Oded	fl. c. 3000	II C 15:1
19. Chanani haRo'eh	fl. c. 3000	II C 16:7
20. Yehu b. Chanani	fl. c. 3000	I K 16:1
21. **Eliyahu haNavi**8	fl. c. 2960-3043	I K 17:1; SO 17, G'ra, 8
22. **Elisha b. Shafat**9	3043-3110	I K 19:16; SO 10, G'ra, 2
23. Ovadiah9a	fl. c. 3030	Ovadiah 1:1, R
24. Michaihu b. Yimlah10	fl. c. 3030	I K 20:13, R; 22:8
25. Yachaziel b. Zechariah	fl. c. 3040	II C 20:14
26. Eliezer b. Dodavahu	fl. c. 3040	II C 20:37

Table XV:
The 48 Prophets of Israel, (cont'd)

Name	Date	Source
27. Yonah b. Amittai	fl. c. 3055	II K 14:25; Jonah 1:1,R
Yehoiada haKohen[15]	fl. c. 3065	II K 11:4
28. Zechariah b. Yehoiada[16]	fl. c. 3080	II C 24:20
29. Amotz (father of Isaiah)[18]	fl. c. 3101-3130	SO 20 on II C 25:7-16
30. Hoshea b. Be'eri[21]	fl. c. 3130-3200	Hoshea 1:1, R
31. Amos[21]	fl. c. 3141-3200	Amos 1:1
32. Isaiah b. Amotz[21 24]	3143-3228	Isaiah 6:1, R; Yev. 49b
33. Michah haMorashti[21]	fl. c. 3168-3200	Michah 1:1; Jer. 26:18
34. Oded	fl. c. 3183-3199	II C 28:9
35. Yoel b. Pesuel[27]	fl. c. 3250	Joel 1:1, R
36. Nachum haElkoshi	fl. c. 3250	Nachum 1:1; II K 21:10,R
37. Chavakuk	fl. c. 3250	Chab. 1:1; II K 21:10, R
38. Zephaniah b. Cushi[28]	fl. c. 3300	Zephaniah 1:1
39. Jeremiah b. Chilkiahu[28 29]	fl. c. 3298-3338	Jeremiah 1:1-3
40. Uriah b. Shemaiahu[32]	fl. c. 3320	Jeremiah 26:20
41. Ezekiel b. Buzi[35]	fl. c. 3327-3338	Ezekiel 1:1-3
[Machseyah] 1(E)[36]**	fl. c. 3330	Megillah 14b
[Neriah] 1(E)[36]**	fl. c. 3330	Megillah 14b
42. Baruch b. Neriah[2]-"D"	fl. c. 3338-3413	Jeremiah 32:12
43. Seraiah b. Neriah[3]-"D"	fl. c. 3350	Jeremiah 51:59
44. Daniel Ish Chamudos[4]-"D"	fl. c. 3340-3400	Dan. 1:6; Meg. 15a
45. Mordecai[6]-"D"	fl. c. 3390-3406	Ezra 2:2, MD; Meg. 15a
46. Chaggai[13]-"D"	3407-3448	Chaggai 1:1, R
47. Zechariah b. Berechiah[13]-"D"	3407-3448	Zechariah 1:1
48. Malachi (Ezra)[13]-"D"	3407-3448	Malachi 1:1; Meg. 15a

*The 48 numbered Prophets in this Table follow Seder Olam, Ch. 20, as emended by the Vilna Gaon. For names and dates of seven Prophetesses of Israel, see Table X

**Names in brackets follow Rashi, Megillah 14a, (s.v. Nevu'ah), who includes Avraham, Yitzchak, Yaakov, Moshe, Aharon, Eli, Shlomo, Neriah, and Machseyah among the forty-eight Prophets, deleting, instead, the three sons of Korach, Assaph, Heiman, Eisan, Yedusun, Zechariah b. Yehoiada, and Daniel. (See Glosses of the G'ra on Megillah 14a, n. 1.)

Names in bold represent the 22 leaders of the chain of Mesorah during this 1,000-year period, as rendered by Maimonides in his Introduction to Mishneh Torah.

Dates preceded by fl. c. are approximate, following the tenure of the Judges and Kings during whose reigns these Prophets are known to have prophesied, as rendered in Tables XIII and XVIII.

For explanatory notes concerning this Table, see Appendix "C." Beginning with Baruch b. Neriah (number 42), explanatory notes will be found in Appendix "D", in Legacy of Sinai."

Legend: C = Chronicles; Ch = Chapter; Chab. = Chabakuk; Dan. = Daniel; Ex. = Exodus; G'ra = Vilna Gaon Commentary; Jer.=Jeremiah; Judg.=Judges; K=Kings; Meg.=Megillah; R=Rashi; S = Samuel; SO = Seder Olam; Yev. = Yevamos.

Table XVI
Time-Line Chart: Era of Torah Centralization

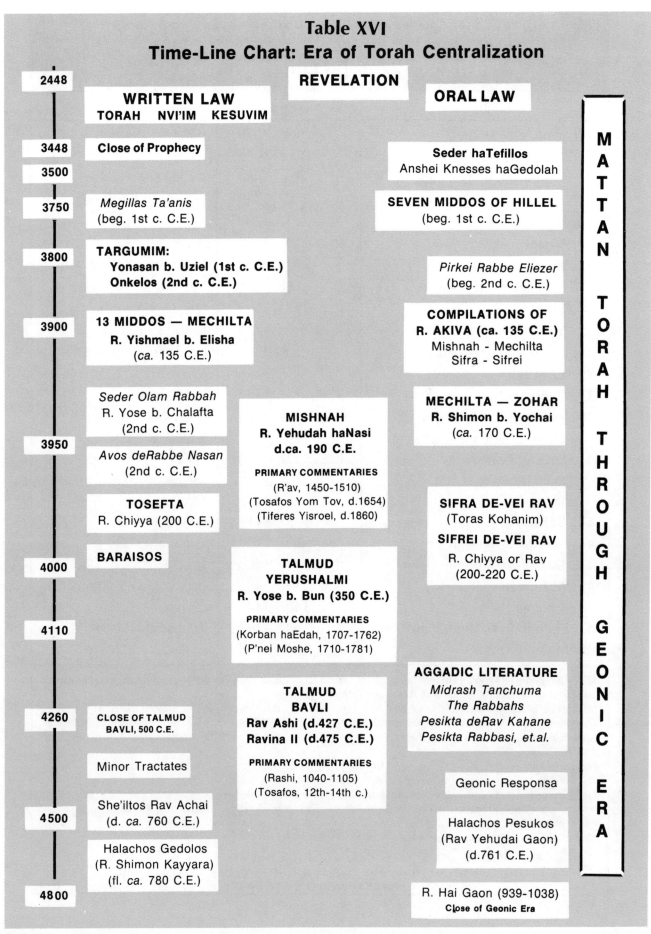

REVELATION

2448			

WRITTEN LAW
TORAH   NVI'IM   KESUVIM

ORAL LAW

3448 — Close of Prophecy

Seder haTefillos
Anshei Knesses haGedolah

3500

3750 — *Megillas Ta'anis*
(beg. 1st c. C.E.)

SEVEN MIDDOS OF HILLEL
(beg. 1st c. C.E.)

3800 — **TARGUMIM:**
   Yonasan b. Uziel (1st c. C.E.)
   Onkelos (2nd c. C.E.)

Pirkei Rabbe Eliezer
(beg. 2nd c. C.E.)

3900 — **13 MIDDOS — MECHILTA**
   R. Yishmael b. Elisha
   (*ca.* 135 C.E.)

COMPILATIONS OF
R. AKIVA (ca. 135 C.E.)
Mishnah - Mechilta
Sifra - Sifrei

Seder Olam Rabbah
R. Yose b. Chalafta
(2nd c. C.E.)

MISHNAH
R. Yehudah haNasi
d.ca. 190 C.E.

PRIMARY COMMENTARIES
(R'av, 1450-1510)
(Tosafos Yom Tov, d.1654)
(Tiferes Yisroel, d.1860)

MECHILTA — ZOHAR
R. Shimon b. Yochai
(*ca.* 170 C.E.)

3950 — *Avos deRabbe Nasan*
(2nd c. C.E.)

TOSEFTA
R. Chiyya (200 C.E.)

SIFRA DE-VEI RAV
(Toras Kohanim)
SIFREI DE-VEI RAV
R. Chiyya or Rav
(200-220 C.E.)

4000 — **BARAISOS**

TALMUD
YERUSHALMI
R. Yose b. Bun (350 C.E.)

PRIMARY COMMENTARIES
(Korban haEdah, 1707-1762)
(P'nei Moshe, 1710-1781)

4110

AGGADIC LITERATURE
Midrash Tanchuma
The Rabbahs
Pesikta deRav Kahane
Pesikta Rabbasi, et.al.

4260 — **CLOSE OF TALMUD**
BAVLI, 500 C.E.

TALMUD
BAVLI
Rav Ashi (d.427 C.E.)
Ravina II (d.475 C.E.)

PRIMARY COMMENTARIES
(Rashi, 1040-1105)
(Tosafos, 12th-14th c.)

Minor Tractates

Geonic Responsa

4500 — She'iltos Rav Achai
(d. *ca.* 760 C.E.)

Halachos Pesukos
(Rav Yehudai Gaon)
(d.761 C.E.)

Halachos Gedolos
(R. Shimon Kayyara)
(fl. *ca.* 780 C.E.)

4800 — R. Hai Gaon (939-1038)
Close of Geonic Era

M A T T A N   T O R A H   T H R O U G H   G E O N I C   E R A

34

Name of Sefer	Redacted by
1-5. Pentateuch	Moshe Rabbbeinu[1]
6. Joshua	Joshua[2]
7. Judges	Samuel[3]
8. Samuel	Samuel, Gad, Nasan[3]
9. Kings	Jeremiah[3a]
10. Isaiah	Anshei Chizkiah[4]
11. Jeremiah	Jeremiah[3a]
12. Ezekiel	Anshei Knesses haGedolah[5]
13. Trei Asar**	Anshei Knesses haGedolah[6]
14. Psalms	King David and Ten Elders[7]
15. Song of Songs	Anshei Chizkiah[8]
16. Ecclesiastes	Anshei Chizkiah[8]
17. Proverbs	Anshei Chizkiah[8]
18. Job	Moshe Rabbeinu[9]
19. Ruth	Samuel[10]
20. Lamentations	Jeremiah[11]
21. Esther	Anshei Knesses haGedolah[5]
22. Daniel	Anshei Knesses haGedolah[5]
23. Ezra - Nechemiah	Ezra[12]
24. Chronicles	Ezra, Nechemiah[12]

This Table follows Bava Basra 14b, 15a.

* For explanatory notes concerning this Table, see Appendix "E," in "Legacy of Sinai." (See also Appendix "C," n. 38.)

** Trei Asar consists of the Twelve Minor Prophets: Hoshea, Yoel, Amos, Ovadiah, Yonah, Michah, Nachum, Chavakkuk, Zephaniah, Chaggai, Zechariah, Malachi.

THE HOUSE OF DAVID

From Shmuel, the Mesorah was transmitted to King David, who was a great Torah scholar, and leader of the Sanhedrin. The Almighty bestowed the mantle of royalty upon David for all generations. King David was succeeded by his son, Solomon, who built the Temple 480 years after the Exodus, in 2928.

The dynasty of David lasted 454 years, from the onset of the reign of King David in the year 2884, until the destruction of the First Temple in the year 3338. During this interval, the following 22 individuals reigned in succession in the Kingdom of Judah. (Asaliah usurped the throne upon the death of her son, Achaziah.)

(1) King David (2) Solomon (3) Rechavam (4) Aviam (5) Asa (6) Yehoshaphat (7) Yehoram (8) Achaziah (9) his mother, Asaliah (10) Yehoash b. Achaziah (11) Amatziah (12) Azariah [Uziah] (13) Yosam (14) Achaz (15) Chizkiah (16) Menasheh (17) Amon (18) Yoshiahu (19) Yehoachaz (20) his brother, Yehoiakim [Eliakim] (21) his son, Yehoiachin [Yechoniah] (22) his uncle, Tzidkiah [Mataniah], during whose reign the Temple was destroyed in 3338.

Among the twenty-one Kings of Judah, King Chizkiah was regarded as the most righteous, second only to King David. During his reign, on Pesach eve 3213, an Angel smote 185,000 men of the army of Sennacherib, King of Assyria, who had besieged Jerusalem, and the Kingdom of Judah was saved from his hands.

The Sages fault Chizkiah for having neglected to sing *shirah*, and to praise G-d for His great deliverance. Had the King not been remiss in this regard, and had he poured forth his heart in thanksgiving to G-d, he would have become the *melech haMashiach*, and his generation would have ushered in the Messianic era.

The Anshei Chizkiah, as the Torah scholars of this generation were known, redacted the prophecies of Isaiah, as well as other Biblical writings.

Symbol of Israel's Eternity

During the reign of Tzidkiah [3338], the Temple of Solomon was destroyed. As the young *Kohanim* threw the keys to the Temple — and then, themselves — into the flames, an outstretched arm reached forth from heaven to snatch the keys from their hands and to lift them heavenward, in a symbolic manifestation of the eternity of Israel.

KINGDOM OF EPHRAIM

During the reign of Rechavam, son of King Solomon, the Ten Tribes of Israel seceded from the Kingdom of Judah, in the year 2964. The Kingdom of Ephraim [the Northern Kingdom], remained an independent Kingdom for 240 years, until the Ten Tribes were exiled by the King of Assyria in 3205.

Unlike in the Kingdom of Judah, the line of succession in the Kingdom of Ephraim was not confined to one particular family group. Rather, the succession of Kings in the Kingdom of Ephraim was a tumultuous one, replete with intrigue, revolutions, conspiracies and assassinations. The following was the line of succession in the Kingdom of Ephraim during the 240-year duration of the Kingdom.

(1) Yeravam b. Nevat (2) his son, Nadav (3) Baasha b. Achiah (4) his son, Elah (5) Zimri (6) Omri/ Tivni (7) Omri (8) his son, Achav (9) his son, Achaziah (10 his brother, Yehoram (11) Yehu b. Yehoshaphat b. Nimshi (12) his son, Yehoachaz (13) his son, Yehoash (14) his son, Yeravam (15) his son, Zechariah (16) Shallum b. Yavesh (17) Menachem b. Gadi (18) his son, Pekachiah (19) Pekach b. Remaliah (20) Hoshea b. Elah, during whose reign the Kingdom of Ephraim was destroyed, and the Ten Tribes led into exile by the King of Assyria, in the year 3205.

Yeravam b. Nevat, the first King of the Kingdom of Ephraim, caused Israel to sin grievously. He set up two Golden Calves in Dan and Bais El, so that the Israelites might no longer look to Jerusalem and to the Kingdom of David as their spiritual and national center. This remained as a stumbling block for the Ten Tribes for the entire 240-year duration of the Kingdom of Ephraim [2964-3205].

The Ten Tribes consisted of Reuven, Shimon, Yisachar, Zevulun, Gad, Asher, Dan, Naftali, Ephraim, and Menasheh. The Tribe of Benjamin remained loyal to the House of David. The *Kohanim* and the Levites, who were scattered throughout Israel, were divided among both Kingdoms.

Except for a small group who returned with Jeremiah in 3303, twenty-five years before the destruction of the First Temple, the whereabouts of the Ten Lost Tribes remain unknown until today.

Table XVIII

*Chronological Table Tracing Mesorah of Prophets According to Kings of Judah and Israel[1], 2884-3338

Kings of Judah** / Kings of Israel	Years of Reign	Dates	Source	Prophets***	During Reign of	Source
King David[1a]	40	2884-2924	II S 5:4-5	Gad	David	I S 22:5; II S 24:11
				Asaph, Yedusun[1b]	David	I C 25:1; II C 35:15
				Heman, Eisan[1b]	David	Ibid.; IC 15:17,19
Solomon[1a]	40	2924-2964	I K 11:42	Nasan[1c]	David, Solomon	II S 7:2; I K 1:11
Construction of First Temple		2928-2934	I K 6:1, 38	Achiah haShiloni[3]	Solomon, Yeravam	I K 6:12; 11:29; S.O. 20
Rechavam	17	2964-2981	I K 14:21	Shemaiah	Rechavam	I K 12:22
Yeravam b. Nevat[2]	22	2964-2985	I K 14:20	Iddo haChozeh	Yeravam	I K 13:1;R; II C 9:29
Aviyam	3	2981-2984	I K 15:2			
Asa	41	2984-3025	I K 15:9-10	Azariah b. Oded	Asa	II C 15:1
Nadav b. Yeravam	2	2985-2986	I K 15:25	Chanani haRo'eh	Asa	II C 16:7
Baasha b. Achiah[4]	24	2986-3009	I K 15:33	Yehu b. Chanani	Baasha	I K 16:1
Elah b. Baasha	2	3009-3010	I K 16:8			
Zimri[5]	7 da.	3010	I K 16:15			
Tivni/Omri[6]	5	3010-3014	I K 16:22			
Omri	7	3014-3021	I K 16:23, R			
Achav b. Omri[7]	22	3021-3042	I K 16:29	Eliyahu haNavi[8]	Achav, Achaziah	I K 17:1; II K 1:15
				Elisha b. Shafat[9]	Achav-Yehoash	I K 19:16; II K 13:20
				Ovadiah[9a]	Yehoshaphat, Achav	Ovadiah 1:1,R
				Michaihu b. Yimlah[10]	Yehoshaphat, Achav	I K 20:13,R; I K 22:8
Yehoshaphat	25	3025-3049	I K 22:42	Yachaziel b. Zechariah	Yehoshaphat	II C 20:14
				Eliezer b. Dodavahu	Yehoshaphat	II C 20:37

Kings of Judah** / Kings of Israel

Kings of Judah** / *Kings of Israel*	Years of Reign	Dates	Source
Achaziah b. Achav	2	3042-3043	I K 22:52
Yehoram b. Achav[11]	12	3043-3055	II K 3:1
Yehoram[12]	8(-2)	3049-3054	II K 8:17
Achaziah b. Yehoram	1	3054-3055	II K 8:26
Asaliah (Yehoram's wife)[13]	6	3055-3061	II K 11:3
Yehu b. Yehoshaphat b.Nimshi[14]	28	3055-3083	II K 10:36
Yehoash b. Achaziah	40	3061-3101	II K 12:2
Yehoachaz b. Yehu	17	3083-3100	II K 13:1
Yehoash b. Yehoachaz[17]	16	3100-3116	II K 13:10,R, M.D.
Amatziah	29	3101-3130	II K 14:2
Yeravam b. Yehoash[19]	41 (-3)	3116-3154	II K 14:23
Azariah (Uziah)[20]	52 (-15)	3130-3168	II K 15:2
			II K 14:22,R
Zechariah b. Yeravam	6 mo.	3154-3155	II K 15:8
Shallum b. Yavesh[22]	1 mo.	3155-3155	II K 15:13
Menachem b. Gadi[22]	10	3155-3165	II K 15:17
Pekachiah b. Menachem[22]	2	3165-3167	II K 15:23

Prophets

Prophets***	During Reign of	Source
Jonah b. Amittai	Yehoram, Yehu	II K 9:1,R; II K 14:25; Jonah 1:1, M
Yehoiada haKohen[15]	Yehoash	II K 11:4
Zechariah b. Yehoiada[16]	Yehoash	II C 24:20
Amotz[18]	Amatziah	S.O. 20, on II C 25:7
Hoshea b. Be'eri[21]	Uziah, Yosam, Achaz, Chizkiah	Hoshea 1:1
Amos[21]	Uziah, Yeravam b. Yehoash	Amos 1:1

* For explanatory notes regarding this Table, see Appendix "C", in "**Legacy of Sinai,**"

** All Kings, except where noted otherwise in Table or Explanatory Notes, were in a direct line of succession, son after son.

*** For the names of other Prophets not mentioned here, see *Seder Olam*, Chaps. 20-21, and Rashi, *Megillah* 14a, *s.v. Nevu'ah she-hutzrechah le-doros;* **See also "Appendix C,"** n. 1, in "**Legacy of Sinai,**" and Table XV.

For sequence of authorship of Torah Nvi'im, and Kesuvim, **see Appendix "C,"** n. 38, in "**Legacy of Sinai,**" and **Table XVII.**

Abbreviations: C = Chronicles; K = Kings; M = Malbim; M.D. = Metzudas David; R = Rashi; S = Samuel; S.O. = Seder Olam Rabbah; S.O.Z. = Seder Olam Zuta

Table XVIII (cont'd) — Tracing Mesorah of Prophets

Kings of Judah / Kings of Israel	Years of Reign	Dates	Source	Prophets	During Reign of	Source
Pekach b. Remaliah[23]	20	3167-3187	II K 15:27	Isaiah[21][24]	Uziah, Yosam,	Isaiah 1:1;
Yosam	16	3168-3183	II K 15:32-33		Achaz, Chizkiah	II K 19:2
Achaz	16	3183-3199	II K 16:2	Michah haMorashti[21]	Yosam, Achaz,	Michah 1:1
					Chizkiah	Jeremiah 26:18
Hoshea b. Elah[25]	18	3187-3205	II K 17:1, 6	Oded	Achaz	II C 28:9
Chizkiah[26]	29	3199-3228	II K 18:2			
Exile of Ten Tribes		3205	II K 18:9-10			
Downfall of Sennacherib		3213	II K 18:13-19:35			
Menasheh	55	3228-3283	II K 21:1	Yoel b. Pesuel[27]	Menasheh	Joel 1:1,R
				Nachum haElkoshi	Menasheh	Nahum 1:1;
						II K 21:10,R
				Chavakkuk	Menasheh	Chavakkuk 1:1;
						II K 21:10,R
Amon	2	3283-3285	II K 21:19	Zephaniah b. Cushi[28]	Yoshiahu	Zephaniah 1:1
Yoshiahu	31	3285-3316	II K 22:1	Jeremiah[29]	Yoshiahu - Tzidkiahu	Jeremiah 1:1-3
Yehoachaz	3 mo.	3316-3316	II K 23:31	Chuldah the Prophetess[30]	Yoshiahu	II K 22:14,R
Yehoiakim (Eliakim)[31]	11	3316-3327	II K 23:36	Uriah b. Shemaiahu[32]	Yehoiakim	Jeremiah 26:20
initial Conquest of Judah		3320	S.O. 24			
Yehoiachin (Yechoniah)[33]	3 mo.	3327	II K 24:8			
Tzidkiahu (Mataniah)[34]	11	3327-3338	II K 24:17-18	Ezekiel[35]	Tzidkiahu-Golah	Ezekiel 1:1-3
Destruction of First Temple		3338	II K 25:8	Machseyah[36]	Tzidkiahu	Megillah 14b
Gedaliah b. Achikam[37]	7 mo.	3338	II K 25:22-25	Neriah[36]	Tzidkiahu	Megillah 14b

Table XIX
Historical Highlights of the Temple Site

I. Significance of the Temple Site.

a. Mikdash shel Ma'alah. The Kodshei haKodoshim — the innter sanctum of the Temple Sanctuary is situated directly beneath the Bais HaMikdash shel Ma'alah — the Heavenly Sanctuary. [Yerushalmi, Berachos 4:5 (35b); Rashi, Genesis 28:17, s.v. Ve-Zeh; Cf. Mechilta on Exodus 15:17.]

b. Even Shesiyah. A large slab of stone at the center of the Kodshei haKodoshim, the Holy of Holies, the Even Shesiyah was the foundation-stone of the earth at the time of creation. [Yoma 54b.]

c. Har haMoriyah. From which Hora'ah — Torah instruction goes forth to the world, and from which Yir'ah — fear of G-d goes forth to the entire world. [Yerushalmi, Berachos 4:5 (35b); Ta'anis 16a; Isaiah 2:2,3.]

d. Bais HaMikdash. Site of Hashra'as haShechinah — manifestation of Divine Presence, equivalent to that which appeared at Sinai. [Ramban, Exodus 25:1.]

e. Kosel Ma'aravi. The Shechinah — the Divine Presence never departed from the Western Wall, even after the Churban. [Tanchuma, Shemos, Piska 10; Zohar 2:4b.]

II. The Temple Mount and the Patriarchs

a. Avraham Avinu. The Temple Mount, or Har haMoriah, was the site of Avraham's tefillah at the time of the Akedah. [Genesis 22:14, R; Pesachim 88a, Rashi, s.v. Har.]

b. Yitzchak Avinu. The Temple Mount was the site of Yitzchak's tefillah, prior to the time when he first met Rivkah. [Genesis 24:63; Pesachim 88a.]

c. Yaakov Avinu. The Temple Mount was the site of Yaakov's tefillah on his road to Charan, and of his dream concerning the ladder which reached heavenward. [Genesis 28:11, R; Pesachim 88a; Sanhedrin 95b.]

III. The Site of the Mizbe'ach — the Sacrificial Altar

a. Man's creation. The site of the Mizbe'ach — the sacrificial altar of atonement — was the site of the creation of Adam haRishon, so that man might be worthy of atonement. [Yerushalmi, Nazir 7:2, p. 35b.]*

b. Adam haRishon. It was also the site of Adam haRishon's first sacrifice, shortly after his creation. [Bereshis Rabbah 34:9; Avodah Zarah 8a.]*

c. Kayin and Hevel. Brought their sacrifices upon this site. [Genesis 4:3-4.]*

d. Noach. Brought his sacrifice here upon his emergence from the Ark. [Genesis 8:20; Yalkut haMakiri, Tehillim 36:5.]*

e. Akedas Yitzchak. Took place upon the site of the Mizbe'ach. [Genesis 22:2, R; Bereshis Rabbah 55:9.]*

f. King David. Purchased this site from Aronah haYevusi, and erected a Mizbe'ach here. [II Samuel 24:25.]*

g. King Solomon. Erected the Temple Mizbe'ach on this site and offered up sacrifices. [I Kings 8:22.]*

h. Anshei Knesses haGedolah. Erected the Mizbe'ach of the Second Temple precisely upon this site, according to the instructions of the Prophets, Chaggai, Zechariah, and Malachi. [Ezra 3:3; Zevachim 62a.]*

* See Pirkei deRabbe Eliezer, Chap. 31; Rambam, Hilchos Bais haBechirah 2:2-4.

Table XX: Seven Tzaddikim[2] Who Encompassed All Generations*

	1	500	1000	1500	2000	2500	3000	3500	4000	4500	5000	5500	6000
ADAM	1- 930												
METHUSELAH	687-1656												
SHEM	1558-2158												
YAAKOV	2108-2255												
AMRAM	2250-2387**												
ACHIAH HaSHILONI	2380-2960**												
ELIYAHU HaNAVI	2960-**...												

*Based upon Bava Basra 121b (See Rashbam, ad. loc.).   ** Dates approximated, according to Rashbam, Bava Basra 121b.

Table XXI: Six Thousand Years of Creation — An Historical Overview*

Two Millennia [Spiritual] Desolation	1-2000	Torah Dissemination [Avraham Avinu]¹
Two Millennia Torah [Dissemination]	2000-4000	Redaction of Mishnah [Rabbeinu haKadosh]²
Two Millennia [Prelude to] Mashiach**	4000-.....	Eliyahu haNavi*** [Herald of Mashiach]³

***"Behold I will send unto you the Prophet, Eliyahu, before the coming of the great and dreadful day of the L-rd."
[Malachi 3:23]

*Based upon Avodah Zarah 9a; Sanhedrin 97a; and Rashi, ad. loc., s.v. U'shnei alpayim Torah.   ²See Legacy of Sinai, Chap. 8, n. 98.   ³See Malachi 3:23.

**See Appendix "A," n. 6, in "Legacy of Sinai."

¹See Appendix "A," n. 6, in "Legacy of Sinai."

THE BABYLONIAN EXILE

The Babylonian King, Nebuchadnezzar, subjugated the Kingdom of Judah and led the Jews into exile in three stages, over an eighteen-year period [3320, 3327, 3338]. Among the exiles were the Prophets Ezekiel and Baruch b. Neriah (disciple of Jeremiah), Daniel, Chananiah, Mishoel, Azariah and Mordecai.

The final exile, in the year 3338, was 850 years after Israel's entry into the land in 2488. During this 850-year period, there were a total of 141 Sabbatical and Jubilee years. Since the Jewish people had desecrated 70 of these Sabbatical years, they were exiled for a corresponding period of 70 years during the First Babylonian Exile.

In 3364, Nebuchadnezzar was succeeded by his son, Evil-Merodach. Twenty-three years later [3386], Evil-Merodach was succeeded by his son, Belshazzar, who reigned for three years.

The guiding spiritual lights during the Babylonian Exile were the Prophets Ezekiel b. Buzi, Baruch b. Neriah, and Daniel Ish Chamudos. During Nebuchadnezzar's reign, Chananiah, Mishoel and Azariah sanctified G-d's Name when they defiantly refused to bow before the King's statue. They were cast into a fiery furnace, from which an Angel rescued them, and they emerged unscathed.

Handwriting on the Wall

In 3389, at a banquet in which he had desecrated the sacred vessels of the Temple, Belshazzar saw the ominous handwriting on the wall. Daniel interpreted the writing as a prediction of Belshazzar's downfall, and the destruction of the mighty Babylonian Empire. That same night, the army of Darius the Mede annihilated the army of Belshazzar, and conquered Babylon.

Darius the Mede reigned one year, during which he cast Daniel into a lion's den, when Daniel refused to discontinue his thrice-daily prayers to the Almighty. Darius bestowed great honor upon Daniel when he emerged unscathed from the lion's den.

The following year marked the ascendancy of the Persian Empire, when Darius was succeeded by Cyrus. During the first year of his reign [3390], Cyrus granted all Jews permission to return to Zion and to rebuild the Temple in Jerusalem.

שיבת ציון — RETURN TO ZION

Led by Zerubbavel b. She'altiel, a descendant of King David, and Yehoshua b. Yehozadak Kohen Gadol, some 42,000 Jews returned jubilantly to Jerusalem to build the Second Temple. After three years, the Samaritans, enemies of the Jews, prevailed upon the King of Persia to withdraw his consent for the Temple construction. Construction of the Temple did not resume until the year 3408.

THE STORY OF PURIM

During this interim period, the story of Purim took place, when Achasuerus succeeded Cyrus as sovereign of the vast dominions of the Persian Empire [3393-3407]. In the seventh year of his reign [3400], Esther was chosen Queen. During Pesach 3404, she appeared before the King to plead with him to nullify Haman's decree. On 13-14 Adar, 3405, the miracle of Purim became a reality.

In the year 3407, Achasuerus was succeeded by his son, Darius II. In the second year of his reign [3408], Darius authorized the completion of the Second Temple. It was completed in 3412.

THE ANSHEI KNESSES HA-GEDOLAH

The spiritual leaders of the Jewish people at the time of the שיבת ציון — the "Return to Zion," were the *Anshei Knesses haGedolah* — the Men of the Great Synod, under the leadership of Ezra haSofer. Included among them were the last of the Prophets, Chaggai, Zechariah and Malachi. *Chazal* observe that Malachi was Ezra. Ezra was the disciple of Baruch b. Neriah, who, in turn, was the disciple of Jeremiah. With the death of Malachi in 3442, the 1,000-year *tekufah* of prophecy came to an end. The *Anshei Knesses haGedolah* composed the basic elements of the *Siddur*.

Shimon haTzaddik, who lived at the time of Alexander the Great, was the last of the *Anshei Knesses haGedolah*. Alexander's conquest of Persia in 3442, brought Eretz Yisroel under Greek dominion. After Alexander's death, his dominions were divided among his four generals, Ptolemy [Egypt], Seleucid [Syria], Antigonos [Asia Minor], and Philip [Macedonia]. At first, Judea came under the Ptolemian dynasty, and later, under the Seleucid dynasty. In 3622, the Chashmonaim overthrew the tyrannical Syrian-Greeks, and the miracle of Chanukah took place.

Table XXII

* First Exile and Construction of the Second Temple, Until the Termination of Prophecy, 3338-3448

Foreign Rule	Tenure	Dates	Source	Prophets	Reign of	Source
Nebuchadnezzar (Babylon)[1]	45 (-19)	3338-3364	S.O. 28;	Baruch b. Neriah[2]	Neb.-Darius II	Jer. 32:21; S.O. 20;
			II Kings 25:8	Seraiah b. Machseyah[3]	Neb.-Darius II	Jer. 51:59; S.O. 20;
Daniel interprets king's dream		3339	Daniel, chap. 2	Daniel[4]	Neb.-Darius II	Dan. 1:6; S.O. 20;
Chananiah, Mishael, Azariah cast into furnace[5]			Daniel, chap. 3			Meg. 15a
Evil-Morodach	23	3364-3386	Daniel 6:1,R;S.O. 28			
Belshazzar	3	3386-3389	Ibid.; Megillah 11b,R			
Daniel deciphers handwriting		3389	Daniel 5:25			
Darius the Mede	1	3389-3390	S.O. 28; Meg. 12a,R			
Daniel in lion's den			Daniel, chap. 6			
Cyrus	3	3390-3392	Ezra 1:1; S.O. 29	Mordecai[6]	Cyrus, Ahasuerus, Darius II	Ezra 2:2, M.D.;
2nd Temple construction begins[7]		3390	Ezra 1:1			Meg. 15a; S.O. 20
Zerubbavel, Yehoshua, Mordecai, ascend to Jerusalem[8]		3390	Ezra 2:2			
Artaxerxes (or Cambyses)[9]	½	3393	Daniel 11:2,R			
Temple construction halted		3393	Ezra 4:7,R			
Ahasuerus	14	3393-3407	S.O. 29	Esther[10]	Ahasuerus	S.O. 21; Meg. 14a
Esther chosen Queen		3400	Esther 2:16			
Daniel advises Esther[11]			Esther 4:5; Meg. 15a			
Mordecai writes Megillah			Esther 9:29,R			
Darius the Persian[12]	35	3406	Ezra 4:24·S.O. 30	Chaggai[13]	Darius II	Chaggai 1:1,R
Temple construction resumes[14]		3407-3442	Ezra 4:24	Zechariah b. Berechiah[13]	Darius II	Zechariah 1:1
Completion of Second Temple		3408	Ezra 6:15	Malachi (Ezra)[15]	Darius II	Malachi 1:1:
Death of Baruch b. Neriah		3412	Megillah 16b			Meg. 15a
Ezra settles in Jerusalem		3413	Ezra 7:7,R; Meg. 16b			
Nechemiah settles in Jerusalem		3413	Nechemiah 1:1,R			
Termination of prophecy		3426	S.O. 30; S.O.Z. 7			
		3442 or				
		3448	Sanhedrin 11a[16]			

* For Explanatory Notes regarding this Chart, see Appendix "D," in "Legacy of Sinai."

45

THE ZUGOS — THE "PAIRS"

Antigonos Ish Socho stood at the head of the *Sanhedrin* after Shimon haTzaddik. Antigonos represents the *Dor haMa'avar* — the Generation of Transition between the *Anshei Knesses haGedolah* and the era of the *Zugos* — the "Pairs."

The *Zugos* consisted of two of the most illustrious Torah scholars of each generation: the *Nasi* — the President, and the *Av Bes Din* — the head of the *Sanhedrin*. The five generations of *Zugos* were: (1) Yose b. Yoezer and Yose b. Yochanan (2) Yehoshua b. Perachiah and Nittai haArbeili (3) Yehudah b. Tabbai and Shimon b. Shetach (4) Shemaiah and Avtalyon (5) Hillel and Shammai

Hillel began his Torah-*Nesi'us* dynasty 100 years before the Second *Churban*. Three years earlier, Herod overthrew the last of the Chashmonean Kings, and established the Herodian Dynasty, with the support of the Roman Emperor, Augustus Caesar. The *Nesi'us* dynasty of Hillel lasted for sixteen generations, until Rabbon Gamliel Basra [429 C.E.], when the Patriarchate was terminated.

THE FIRST GENERATION OF TANNAIM

The disciples of Hillel and Shammai were among the earliest *Tannaim*. They included such illustrious personalities as Rabbon Shimon b. Hillel and his son Rabbon Gamliel haZaken; Yonasan b. Uziel, and Rabbon Shimon b. Gamliel who was put to death at the time of the *Churban*.

Rabbon Yochanan b. Zakkai was head of the Sanhedrin during the *Churban* in 68 C.E. At great peril to himself, he prevailed upon the Roman conqueror, Vespasian, to grant him "the city of Yavneh, and its Torah scholars," and he transferred the Sanhedrin from Jerusalem to Yavneh. Rabbon Gamliel II presided in Yavneh after the *Churban*.

THE SECOND GENERATION OF TANNAIM

The 5 most illustrious disciples of Rabbon Yochanan b. Zakkai in the Second Generation of *Tannaim* were: (1) Rabbe Eliezer b. Hyrcanus; (2) Rabbe Yehoshua b. Chananiah; (3) Rabbe Yose ha-Kohen; (4) Rabbe Shimon b. Nesanel; (5) Rabbe Elazar b. Arach.

Among the other leading scholars of this generation were: Rabbe Chanina b. Dosa, Rabbe Elazar b. Zadok, Nachum Ish Gamzu, and Rabbe Nechuniah b. haKanah.

THE THIRD GENERATION OF TANNAIM

Rabbe Akiva was the greatest disciple of Rabbe Yehoshua and Rabbe Eliezer. Some of his illustrious colleagues during the Third Generation were: Rabbe Yishmael b. Elisha II, who compiled the *Mechilta;* Rabbe Tarfon; Rabbe Yose haGelili; and Rabbe Elazar b. Azariah, a tenth generation descendant of Ezra haSofer.

Rabbe Akiva, who died as a martyr after the unsuccessful revolt of Bar Kochba and the fall of Betar in 135 C.E., set the groundwork for the redaction of the Mishnah by Rabbe Yehudah haNasi, two generations later. Also among the *Asarah Harugei Malchus* — the Ten Martyred Scholars of the Hadrianic persecutions were: Rabbe Chanina b. Teradyon, who was burned together with a *Sefer Torah,* and Rabbe Yehudah b. Bava, who was slain while giving *semichah* to five of Rabbe Akiva's greatest *talmidim.*

THE FOURTH GENERATION OF TANNAIM

The five outstanding disciples of Rabbe Akiva who were ordained by Rabbe Yehudah b. Bava, and who were known as *Rabbosenu she-be-Darom* — our teachers of the South, were: (a) Rabbe Meir; (b) Rabbe Yehudah bar Ilai; (c) Rabbe Shimon b. Yochai; (d) Rabbe Yose b. Chalafta and (e) Rabbe Elazar b. Shammua. Some include Rabbe Nechemiah in this group.

Rabbe Shimon b. Yochai was the author of the *Zohar* and of the *Mechilta Achariti* — the "other" *Mechilta* which had been lost for many centuries. Rabbon Shimon b. Gamliel II was the *Nasi* at this time, while Rabbe Meir was the *Chacham Bais haVa'ad,* and Rabbe Nasan haBavli was the *Av Bes Din.*

RABBEINU HA-KADOSH — REDACTION OF THE MISHNAH

The most illustrious Torah master of the fifth and last generation of *Tannaim* was Rabbe Yehudah haNasi, a direct sixth generation descendant of the *Nesi'us* dynasty of Hillel haZaken. Better known as Rabbeinu haKadosh or simply as Rebbe, Rabbe Yehudah haNasi redacted the Mishnah in approximately 188 C.E. [3948], 500 years after the termination of prophecy in the year 3448.

The redaction of the Mishnah by Rebbe and his *Sanhedrin* marked a monumental milestone in the history of Torah transmission. The Mishnah is the vast repository and the definitive authoritative source of the accumulated wisdom of the Oral Law, which was transmitted to Moshe at Sinai.

Table XXIII — Chain of Mesorah
From Ezra to Hillel haZaken, 3390-3768

Anshei Knesses haGedolah — Ezra and his Sanhedrin

Chaggai, Zechariah, Malachi, Daniel, Chananiah, Mishael, Azariah, Nechemiah, Mordecai, Zerubbavel, Yehoshua b. Yehozadak, Seraiah, Re'eilayah, et. al. (120 Prophets and Sages), *Arranged order of tefillos; Closed Biblical Canon; Reviewed Masores; Classified Oral Law.*

Cyrus authorizes construction of Second Temple — 3390; Temple construction interrupted — 3393; Ahasuerus, Story of Purim [3393-3407]; Construction of Second Temple resumes under Darius II (b. Esther) [3408-3412].

Ezra settles in Jerusalem — 3413; Death of Chaggai, Zechariah, Malachi (Ezra), Termination of prophecy - 3448 (1,000 years after Mattan Torah).

Close of Era of Anshei Knesses HaGedolah

Shimon haTzaddik *[greets Alexander the Great, 3448]; Minyan Shetaros begins.*

Generation of Transition between Anshei Knesses haGedolah and Zugos

Antigonos of Socho; [R. Elazar b. Charsom]; *Targum Shiv'im (Septuagint — Ptolemy Philadelphus), 3515; Emergence of Sadducees and Boethusians.*

Five Generations of Zugos

1. Yose b. Yoezer of Zeredah and Yose b. Yochanan of Jerusalem; [Mattisyahu b. Yochanan Kohen Gadol].
2. Yehoshua b. Perachyah and Nittai haArbeli; [Yochanan b. Mattisyahu]. *Yehudah haMaccabbe; Chashmonean Dynasty, 3622-3725 (103 years).*
3. Yehudah b. Tabbai and Shimon b. Shetach; [Choni haMe'aggel, Elyehoenai b. haKof]. *Reign of Alexander Yannai and Queen Sh'lomis Alexandra.*
4. Shemaiah and Avtalyon; [Akavyah b. Mahalalel; Admon; Chanan b. Avishalom; R. Mayasha]. *Civil strife between Hyrcanus II and Aristobolus II, sons of Alexander Yannai.*
5. Hillel and Shammai, *Seven Middos of Hillel haZaken, Presidency of Hillel, 3728-3768;* [Benei Basyra; Menachem; Chananiah b. Chizkiah b. Garon, *Megillas Ta'anis, Elucidated Book of Ezekiel]. Herod the Idumean, 3725-3764.*

★   ★   ★   ★   ★   ★   ★   ★

Kings of Chashmonean Dynasty, 3622-3725 (138-35 B.C.E.—103 years)

(a) Mattisyahu b. Yochanan *[Yose b. Yoezer]* **(b)** Yehudah haMaccabee (his son); *Chanukah [Yehoshua b. Perachyah]* **(c)** Yonasan b. Mattisyahu (Yehudah's brother) **(d)** Shimon b. Mattisyahu (another brother) **(e)** Yochanan Hyrcanus b. Shimon **(f)** Aristobolus b. Yochanan Hyrcanus **(g)** Alexander Yannai b. Yochanan Hyrcanus *[Shimon b. Shetach]* **(h)** Sh'lomis Alexandra (wife of Alexander Yannai and sister of Shimon b. Shetach) **(i)** Aristobolus II and **(j)** Hyrcanus II (her sons) *[Shemaiah and Avtalyon]; Pompey conquers Jerusalem, 63 B.C.E.* **(k)** Antigonos b. Aristobolus.

Herodian Dynasty — 3725-3828 (35 B.C.E.-68 C.E. — 103 years)

(a) Herod the Great, son of Antipater the Idumean (35 B.C.E.-4 C.E.) **(b)** his three sons, Archelaus (Judea); Philip (Caesaria — Phillipi); Herod Antipas (4 C.E.-37 C.E., Tiberias); *Judea becomes Roman province—6 C.E.; Concurrent rule of Roman procurators* **(c)** Agrippa I [grandson of Herod] (37-44 C.E.) **(d)** Agrippa II [his son], (48-68 C.E.); *68 C.E. — Second Temple Destroyed.*

Table XXIV — Chain of Mesorah
The Tannaitic Era, 3768-3960

First Generation of Tannaim — ca. 3770-3830 (10-70 C.E.)

R. Shimon b. Hillel haZaken; Bais Shammai and Bais Hillel; R. Gamliel haZaken; Yonasan b. Uziel, *Targum Yonasan on Nvi'im;* R. Yishmael b. Elisha I, Kohen Gadol; R. Shimon b. Gamliel I (d. 68 C.E.); R. Yochanan b. Zakkai.

Abba Shaul b. Botnis; Bava b. Buta; Ben Hei Hei; R. Chananiah S'gan haKohanim; R. Dosa b. Harkinas; Dostai of Kefar Yasmah; Elazar b. Chananiah; R. Eliezer b. Yaakov I; Nachum haLavler; Nachum haMadai; R. Shimon ish haMitzpah; R. Yehoshua b. Gamla, Kohen Gadol, *Established Torah school network;* R. Yehudah b. Basyra I; R. Yochanan b. Bag Bag; R. Yochanan b. haChoranis; R. Zadok; R. Zechariah b. haKetzav.
Destruction of Second Temple — 3828 (68 C.E.).

Second Generation of Tannaim — ca. 3830-3870 (70-110 C.E.)

R. Yochanan b. Zakkai; R. Gamliel of Yavneh; *R. Eliezer b. Hyrcanus (R. Eliezer haGadol), *Pirkei de Rabbe Eliezer,* *R. Yehoshua b. Chananiah; *R. Yose haKohen; *R. Shimon b. Nesanel; *R. Elazar b. Arach; [*Disciples of R. Yochanan b. Zakkai].

R. Chaninah b. Dosa; R. Elazar b. Zadok I; Nachum Ish Gamzo; R. Nechunya b. haKanah; R. Papiyas; Shimon achi Azariah; R. Shimon b. haSagan; Shimon haPakuli, *Arranged the Eighteen Benedictions;* Shmuel haKattan, *Birchas haMinim;* R. Yochanan b. Gudgeda.

Third Generation of Tannaim — ca. 3870-3895 (110-135 C.E.)

*R. Akiva b. Yosef, *Began compilation of Mishnah, Mechilta, Sifra, Sifrei;* *R. Yishmael b. Elisha, *Thirteen Hermeneutic Principles, Mechilta of R. Yishmael;* [*The Two Schools of Halachic Midrash]; R. Tarfon; R. Yose haGelili; R. Elazar b. Azariah (tenth generation descendant of Ezra); *R. Chananiah b. Teradyon; *R. Chanina b. Chachinai; *R. Chutzpis haMeturgeman; *R. Yehudah b. Bava; *R. Yehudah haNachtom; *R. Yeshevav haSofer; [*included among Asarah Harugei Malchus].

Abba Shaul; R. Chalafta; Chanan haMitzri; R. Chananiah b. achi R. Yehoshua; R. Chanina b. Antigonos; R. Chanina ish Ono; R. Elazar b. Damah; R. Elazar b. Masya; R. Elazar b. Parta; R. Elazar Chisma; R. Elazar haModa'i; R. Ilai haZaken; R. Masya b. Cheresh; Onkelos, *Targum Onkelos on Torah;* Shimon b. Azzai; R. Shimon b. Nanas; Shimon b. Zoma; Shimon haTimni; R. Yehoshua haGarsi; R. Yehudah b. Basyra II; R. Yochanan b. Beroka; R. Yochanan b. Nuri; R. Yochanan B. Torta; R. Yose b. Kisma.
Bar Kochba Era and Fall of Betar, 130-135 C.E.

Fourth Generation of Tannaim — ca. 3895-3930 (135-170 C.E.)

*R. Meir; *R. Yehudah b. Ilai; *R. Shimon b. Yochai, *Zohar, Mechilta;* *R. Yose b. Chalafta, *Seder Olam;* *R. Elazar b. Shammua; *R. Nechemiah; [*Disciples of Rabbe Akiva, ordained by R. Yehudah b. Bava]; Rabbon Shimon b. Gamliel II.

Table XXIV (cont'd)

Fourth Generation of Tannaim (cont'd)

Abba Chanan; R. Chananiah b. Akavyah; R. Chanina b. Gamliel; R. Elazar b. Zadok II; R. Eliezer b. Yaakov II; R. Eliezer b. R. Yose haGelili, *32 Hermeneutic Principles of Midrashic Exegesis;* R. Nasan haBavli, *Avos deRabbe Nasan;* R. Pereida; R. Shimon Shezuri; R. Yaakov b. Korshai; R. Yehoshua b. Korcha; R. Yishmael b. R. Yochanan b. Beroka; R. Yitzchak; R. Yochanan haSandelar; R. Yonasan; R. Yoshiah.

Fifth and Final Generation of Tannaim — ca. 3930-3960 (170-200 C.E.)

R. Yehudah haNasi (Rabbeinu haKadosh), *Redaction of Mishnah, 3948 (188 C.E., 1500 years after Mattan Torah).*

R. Chiyya Rabbah, *Tosefta;* R. Dostai b. Yannai; R. Elazar b. R. Shimon b. Yochai; R. Elazar b. R. Yose; R. Elazar haKappar; Issi b. Yehudah; R. Menachem b. R. Yose; R. Pinchas b. Yair; R. Shimon b. Chalafta; R. Shimon b. Elazar; R. Shimon b. Menasya; R. Shimon b. Yehozadak; R. Shimon b. Yehudah; R. Simai; Sumchus; R. Yehudah b. Lakish; R. Yishmael b. R. Yose; R. Yose b. haMeshulam; R. Yose b. R. Yehudah.

Many Tannaim may be classified in one of two or more generations. This will account for variations which may occur on various charts of this era.

Table XXV — Roman Emperors During Tannaitic Era

63 B.C.E.	Pompey the Great conquers Jerusalem
	Judea comes under Roman rule
59 B.C.E.	First Triumvirate: Pompey, Caesar, Cassius
44 B.C.E.	Julius Caesar assassinated
42 B.C.E.	Second Triumvirate: Antony, Lepidus, Octavian
35 B.C.E.	**Herodian Dynasty Era of Hillel haZaken**
27 B.C.E.-14 C.E.	August Caesar (Octavian) — First Emperor
14 C.E.-37 C.E.	Tiberius
6 C.E.	**Judea becomes Roman Province**
	Concurrent rule of Roman procurators begins
	Zealot sect (Biryonim) forms resistance
37- 41 C.E.	Gaius Caligula 41-54 C.E. Claudius
54- 68 C.E.	Nero 69 C.E. Galbo; Otho; Vitellius
69- 79 C.E.	Vespasian *[Rabbon Yochanan ben Zakkai]*
70 C.E.	**Second Temple Destroyed**
73 C.E.	*Fall of Masada*
79- 81 C.E.	Titus 81-96 C.E. Domitian 96-98 C.E. Nerva
98-117 C.E.	Trajan 117-138 C.E. Hadrian
132-135 C.E.	**Bar Kochba Revolt**
135 C.E.	*Fall of Betar*
	Rabbe Akiva Asarah Harugei Malchus
138-161 C.E.	Antoninus Pius
161-181 C.E.	Marcus Aurelius *[Rabbeinu haKadosh]*
188 C.E.	*Redaction of Mishnah*
350 C.E.	*Completion of Talmud Yerushalmi*
360-363 C.E.	Julianus the Apostate
	Permanent Jewish Calendar — Cessation of Sanhedrin
476 C.E.	Fall of Roman Empire

For sources and explanatory notes regarding this Table, See Legacy, Chap. VIII.

THE TEN LOCATIONS OF THE SANHEDRIN

The Talmud observes, that, because of Roman persecution, the seat of the Sanhedrin was "exiled" to ten different locations, after it was removed from the *Lishkas haGazis,* the Temple Assembly Hall, which was its permanent location.

The Sanhedrin was exiled (a) from the Lishkas haGazis to Chanus [a location on the Temple Mount] (b) from Chanus to Jerusalem (c) from Jerusalem to Yavneh (d) from Yavneh to Usha [a city in the Galil] (e) from Usha to Yavneh (f) from Yavneh to Usha (g) from Usha to Shefaram (h) from Shefaram to Bais She'arim (i) from Bais She'arim to Sepphoris (j) from Sepphoris to Tiberias

The following table provides the names of the *Nesi'im,* as well as the names of the Roman emperors, during whose dynasties this transition of the Sanhedrin took place.

Table XXVI
The Sanhedrin and the Nesi'im during the Tannaitic Era

Hillel haZaken, 32 B.C.E.-8 C.E., *Lishkas haGazis* [Second Triumvirate, 44-27 B.C.E.; Octavian, 27 B.C.E.-14 C.E.] *(Herod, 35 B.C.E.- 4 C.E.).*

Rabbon Shimon b. Hillel, ca. 8-15 C.E., *Lishkas haGazis* [Octavian, d.14 C.E.] (3 sons of Herod, 4-37 C.E.).

Rabbon Gamliel haZaken, ca. 15- 48 C.E., *Lishkas haGazis; (a) Chanus; (b) Jerusalem* [Tiberius, 14-37 C.E.; Caligula, 37- 41 C.E.] *(3 Sons of Herod, 4-37 C.E.; Agrippa I, 37- 44 C.E.).*

Rabbon Shimon b. Gamliel I, ca. 48-68 C.E., *(b) Jerusalem* [Claudius, 41-54 C.E.; Nero, 54-68 C.E.] *(Agrippa II, 48-68 C.E.), Second Churban.*

Rabbon Yochanan b. Zakkai, d.ca. 78 C.E. *(c) Yavneh.* **Rabbon Gamliel II, of Yavneh,** d.ca. 120 C.E. *(c) Yavneh; (d) Usha; (e) Yavneh.* (Rabbe Elazar b. Azariah, *Lud.*) [Vespasian, 69-79 C.E.; Titus, 79-81; Domitian, 81-96; Nerva, 96-98; Trajan, 98-117; Hadrian, 117-138 C.E.]. Rabbe Akiva, d.135 C.E. *(f) Usha. Bar Kochba Revolt,* 132-135 C.E.

Rabbon Shimon b. Gamliel II, ca. 125-160 C.E. *(f) Usha (g) Shefaram* [Hadrian, 117-138 C.E.; Antoninus Pius, 138-161 C.E.]. שלפי השמד — *Aftermath of "Shmad."*

Rabbe Yehudah haNasi, ca. 160-195 C.E. *(h) Bais She'arim; (i) Sepphoris; (j) Tiberias* [Marcus Aurelius, 161-181 C.E.]; Commodus, 181-192 C.E.; *Redaction of Mishnah,* ca. 188 C.E.- 1500 years after Mattan Torah.

For sources, see Legacy of Sinai, p. 165, nn. 43-46; See also Rosh Hashanah 31a-b.

Note: The symbols (a) through (j) represent the ten locations to which the Sanhedrin was exiled from its permanent site in the "Lishkas haGazis" [an assembly hall in the Temple]. (a) Chanus [on the Temple Mount, but not in the Temple proper]; (b) Jerusalem; (c) Yavneh; (d) Usha; (e) Yavneh II; (f) Usha II; (g) Shefaram; (h) Bais She'arim; (i) Sepphoris (j) Tiberias.
See Rosh Hashanah 31a-b, Rashi, ad. loc.; See also Legacy, p. 165, nn. 43-46; p. 176, n. 98.

DOR HA-MA'AVAR — GENERATION OF TRANSITION

Some of the leaders of the Generation of Transition between the *Tannaim* and *Amoraim* were Rabbe Chiyya, who wrote the *Tosefta*; his sons, Yehudah and Chizkiah; Rabbe Effes; Rabbe Chanina bar Chama; Rabbe Gamliel and Rabbe Shimon, sons of Rebbe; Levi bar Sisi; and in Bavel, Avuha diShmuel, the father of Shmuel.

THE EARLY BABYLONIAN AMORAIM

The close of the Mishnah and the era of the *Tannaim* [ca. 200 C.E.], ushered in the era of the *Amoraim*, which lasted 300 years, until the close of the Babylonian Talmud in 500 C.E. The *Tannaim* functioned primarily in Eretz Yisroel, despite the turbulent and even precarious conditions which often prevailed there under Roman rule, which was tyrannical and despotic more often than it was benevolent. The activity of the *Amoraim*, on the other hand, took place both in Bavel and in Eretz Yisroel, and culminated with the redaction of the *Talmud Yerushalmi* in Eretz Yisroel [ca. 350 C.E.], and the *Talmud Bavli* in Bavel [ca. 500 C.E.].

In 219 CE. [3979] Rav, an outstanding disciple of Rabbeinu haKadosh and nephew of Rabbe Chiyya, descended to Bavel, and established a Yeshiva in Sura [219-247], while his great colleague, Shmuel, stood at the head of a Yeshiva in Nehardea [219-254 C.E.]. In 254 C.E., Rav Huna, illustrious disciple of Rav and Shmuel, relocated the Academy of Sura in nearby Masa Machsya.

Shortly after Shmuel's death in 4014 [254 C.E.], Nehardea was destroyed by the Tadmurs. Whereupon, Rav Yehudah b. Yechezkel [d. 299 C.E.], another great disciple of Rav and Shmuel, re-established Shmuel's academy in Pumbedisa, where it soon rivaled the Torah splendor of the academies of Sura and Masa Machsya.

RABBE YOCHANAN AND THE TALMUD YERUSHALMI

At this time, Rabbe Yochanan bar Napcha, one of the youngest disciples of Rabbeinu haKadosh, stood at the head of Rebbe's Yeshiva in Tiberias. During the six decades of Rabbe Yochanan's tenure as *Rosh Yeshiva* [228-288 C.E.], Rabbe Yochanan established the foundations of the *Talmud Yerushalmi*.

The *Talmud Yerushalmi* was not redacted and completed, however, until some six decades after the death of Rabbe Yochanan, in 352 C.E., under Rabbe Manna b. Rabbe Yonah, and Rabbe Yose bar Bun, during the fifth and last generation of Palestinian *Amoraim*.

THE ERETZ YISROEL AMORAIM

The following was the succession of Torah leadership in the Eretz Yisroel academies.

Resh Lakish was Rabbe Yochanan's great *talmid-chaver* — disciple-colleague. Rabbe Yochanan and Resh Lakish were succeeded, first by Rabbe Eliezer b. Pedas, and then by Rabbe Ammi and Rabbe Assi, of the third generation of Palestinian *Amoraim*. They were suceeded, in turn, by Rabbe Yirmiyah, Rabbe Chaggai, Rabbe Avin, Rabbe Yonah, and Rabbe Yose of the fourth generation of Palestinian *Amoraim*. Rabbe Mana and Rabbe Yose bar Bun led the fifth and last generation of Palestinian *Amoraim*.

Due to incessant persecution by the Christian-Roman Emperors, who had adopted Christianity as the official State-religion during the reign of Constantine [307-337], the Eretz Yisroel academies of Tiberias, Caesaria, and later Sepphoris, were forced to close [ca. 352 C.E.]. The remaining Palestinian *Amoraim* fled to Bavel.

Hillel haSheni and the Jewish Calendar

A few years later, during a brief respite for the Jews under Julianus Caesar [361-363 C.E.], Hillel the Second — a thirteenth generation descendant of Hillel haZaken, established the permanent Jewish calendar. Immediately after the death of Julianus, the persecutions resumed with far greater intensity. The remaining Palestinian *Amoraim* fled to Bavel, and it was not long before the *Sanhedrin* ceased to function entirely.

LATER BABYLONIAN AMORAIM

In the academies of Bavel, first Rabbah bar Nachmani, and then his colleague, Rav Yosef, succeeded Rav Yehudah b. Yechezkel as *Roshei Yeshiva* of Pumbedisa. During the tenure of Rabbah bar Nachmani, as many as 12,000 students attended the twice-annual *Yarchei Kallah* sessions in Pumbedisa.

Rabbah and Rav Yosef were succeeded, in turn, by Abbaye [d. 338 C.E.] and Rava [d. 352 C.E.], as *Roshei Yeshiva* in Pumbedisa. During Rava's tenure, the academy of Pumbedisa was moved to Rava's city of Mechoza. Rava's death in 352 C.E. coincided approximately with the deaths of Rabbe Mana and Rabbe Yose bar Bun in Eretz Yisroel, and the close of the *Talmud Yerushalmi*.

RAV ASHI — REDACTION OF THE TALMUD BAVLI

Not long after the death of Rava in 352 C.E., the 6th generation Babylonian *Amora*, Rav Ashi, became *Rosh Yeshiva* in Masa Machsya. During the 56-year tenure of Rav Ashi as *Rosh Yeshiva* [371-427 C.E.], his academy at Masa Machsya was regarded as the central Torah Academy of all Israel. Under Rav Ashi, the *Talmud Bavli* was compiled and redacted, much as the Mishnah had been redacted by Rabbeinu haKadosh almost 240 years earlier. The Babylonian Talmud was not closed entirely, however, until the earliest decades of the *Rabbanan Savorai*, in 500 C.E.

EIGHTEEN GENERATIONS — FROM EZRA TO RAV ASHI

The Rambam cites the names of the following illustrious Torah scholars who stood at the helm of the Jewish community, in an uninterrupted succession of Torah leadership, from the era of Ezra until the redaction of the Babylonian Talmud by Rav Ashi.

(1) Shimon haTzaddik (2) Antigonos of Socho (3) Yose b. Yoezer and Yosef b. Yochanan (4) Yehoshua b. Perachiah and Nittai haArbeli (5) Yehudah b. Tabbai and Shimon b. Shetach (6) Shemaiah and Avtalyon (7) Hillel and Shammai (8) Rabbon Shimon b. Hillel (9) Rabbon Gamliel haZaken (10) Rabbon Shimon b. Gamliel (11) Rabbon Gamliel II (12) Rabbon Shimon b. Gamliel II (13) Rabbeinu haKadosh (14) Rav; Shmuel; Rabbe Yochanan (15) Rav Huna (16) Rabbah and Rav Yosef (17) Abbaye and Rava (18) Rav Ashi

THE RABBANAN SAVORAI

The Babylonian Talmud was closed in 500 C.E., during the early decades of the *Rabbanan Savorai*. After that date, the *Rabbanan Savorai*, who were מקרבי להוראה — close to the era of halachic determination of the *Amoraim*, were no longer authorized to make emendations within the Talmudic text. The era of the *Rabbanan Savorai* lasted 115 years [475-589 C.E.], terminating with Rav Giza and Rav Sama, who led the last generation of *Rabbanan Savorai*.

During the closing decades of the *Rabbanan Savorai*, ever-increasing persecutions under the Neo-Persian Sasanid Kings forced both Yeshivos of Sura and Pumbedisa to close for about thirty years. The Sages fled to Peroz-Shavor, near Nehardea, which was under the far more benevolent Arab rule. It was in the Academy of Peroz-Shavor that the Minor Tractates were redacted.

Table XXVII

Chronological Table of Amoraim
and Rabbanan Savorai: 3960-4350 (200-590 C.E.)

Generation of Transition between Tannaim and Amoraim — 3960-3980 (200-220 C.E.)

Eretz Yisroel: Sons of R. Yehudah haNasi — Rabbon Gamliel III and R. Shimon; Sons of R. Chiyya Rabbah — Yehudah and Chizkiah; Bar Kappara, *Baraisos;* Levi bar Sisi, *Baraisos;* R. Yonasan b. Amram.

Bavel: Abba bar Abba, father of Shmuel; R. Huna I, the Exilarch; R. Shila.

First Generation of Amoraim — ca. 3980-4040 (220-250 C.E.)

Eretz Yisroel: R. Efess [Sepphoris]; R. Chanina bar Chama [Sepphoris]; R. Oshaya Rabbah [Caesarea], *Baraisos*; R. Yannai; R. Yehoshua b. Levi [Lydda]; R. Yehudah Nesiah I; R. Yonasan b. Elazar.

Bavel: Rav (R. Abba Aricha b. Aivu), *founded Sura 3979,* d. 4007 (219-247 C.E.), *Sifra, Sifrei;* Shmuel [Nehardea], 3979-4014 (219-254 C.E.); Mar Ukva, the Exilarch; Karna, Dayyan haGolah; Rav Kahana I; Rabbah b. Chana.

Second Generation of Amoraim — ca. 4010-4050 (250-290 C.E.)

Eretz Yisroel: R. Yochanan b. Naphcha [Tiberias], 3988-4048 (228-288 C.E.), *Laid foundations of Talmud Yerushalmi*; R. Shimon b. Lakish (Resh Lakish); R. Simlai; R. Yitzchak Naphcha; R. Yaakov b. Idi; R. Ze'iri; R. Elazar b. Pedas [Tiberias], d. 4048 (288 C.E.); Ilfa.

Bavel: R. Huna [Masa Machsya — Sura], 4017-4057 (257-297 C.E.); R. Yehudah b. Yechezkel [Pumbedisa], 4017-4059 (257-299 C.E.); Rabbah b. Avuha [Nehar.], 4014-4019 (254-259 C.E.) [and Mechoza]; R. Chisda [Sura], 4053-4069 (293-309 C.E.); R. Sheshes [Shilchi]; R. Nachman bar Yaakov [Mechoza]; R. Ada b. Ahavah; Rami b. Yechezkel; R. Hamnuna I.

Third Generation of Amoraim — ca. 4050-4080 (290-320 C.E.)

Eretz Yisroel: R. Ammi [Tiberias]; R. Assi; R. Shmuel bar Nachmani; Rabbah bar bar Chana; R. Chiyya bar Abba; Ula; R. Abbahu [Caesarea]; R. Zeira I; R. Levi; R. Chanina bar Papa; R. Abba bar Kahana; R. Ilai.

Bavel: Rabbah b. Nachmani [Pumb.], 4059-4080 (299-320 C.E.); R. Yosef (b. Chiyya) [Pumb.], 4080-4083 (320-323 C.E.), *Targum on Chronicles;* R. Yosef b. Chama (father of Rava); Rabbah b. R. Huna [Sura], 4069-4080 (309-320 C.E.); R. Huna b. Chiyya [Pumb.]; R. Hamnuna II; Rabbah b. R. Nachman.

Fourth Generation of Amoraim — ca. 4080-4110 (320-350 C.E.)

Eretz Yisroel: R. Yirmiyah; R. Chaggai [Tib.]; R. Yonah [Tib.]; R. Yose [Tib.]; R. Avin (Ravin).

Bavel: Abbaye [Pumb.], 4086-4098 (326-338 C.E.); Rava [Mechoza — Pumb.], 4098-4112 (338-352 C.E.); R. Nachman bar Yitzchak [Pumb.], 4112-4116 (352-356 C.E.); Rami bar Chama; R. Zeira II; R. Ada bar Abba; R. Nachman b. R. Chisda; R. Dimi.

Table XXVII (cont'd)

Amoraim and Rabbanan Savorai

Fifth Generation of Amoraim — ca. 4110-4145 (350-385 C.E.)

Eretz Yisroel: R. Mana b. R. Yonah [Sepphoris], d. ca. 4112; R. Avin b. R. Avin; R. Yose bar Bun, **Redaction of Talmud Yerushalmi,** completed ca. 4110 (350 C.E.); R. Tanchuma b. Abba, *Midrash Tanchuma*; Hillel II b. Yehudah Nesiah III (13th generation descendant of Hillel haZaken) *Arranged permanent calendar, 4119 (359 C.E.); Cessation of Sanhedrin.*

Bavel: R. Papa [Naresh — Sura], 4112-4131 (352-371 C.E.); R. Huna b'rei deRav Yehoshua; R. Mesharsheya; R. Chama [Nehardea — Pumb.], 4116-4137 (356-377 C.E.); R. Zevid [Pumb.], 4137-4145 (377-385 C.E.); R. Dimi of Nehardea [Pumb.], 4145-4148 (385-388 C.E.).

Sixth Generation of Amoraim — ca. 4145-4185 (385-425 C.E.)

Bavel: Ameimar [Sura]; Ravina I; R. Ashi [Masa Machsya], 4131-4187 (371-427 C.E.), **Redaction of Talmud Bavli;** Meremar [Sura], 4187-4192 (427-432 C.E.); R. Yeimar; Rafram bar Papa II [Pumb.], 4148-4155 (388-395 C.E.); R. Kahana V [Pumb.], 4155-4174 (395-414 C.E.); Mar Zutra [Pumb.], 4174-4176 (414-416 C.E.); R. Acha b'rei deRava [Pumb.], 4176-4179 (416-419 C.E.); R. Geviha of Bei Kasil [Pumb.], 4179-4193 (419-433 C.E.); Rafram of Pumbedisa [Pumb.], 4193-4203 (433-443 C.E.).

Seventh Generation of Amoraim — ca. 4185-4220 (425-460 C.E.)

Bavel: R. Idi bar Avin II [Sura], 4192-4212 (432-452 C.E.); R. Nachman b. R. Huna [Sura], 4212-4215 (452-455 C.E.); Mar bar R. Ashi (R. Tavyumi) [Masa Machsya — Sura], 4215-4228 (455-468 C.E.); R. Acha bar Rav; R. Richomi II [Pumbedisa], 4203-4216 (443-456 C.E.); R. Sama b'rei deRava [Pumb.], 4216-4236 (456-476 C.E.).

Eighth and Final Generation of Amoraim — ca. 4220-4235 (460-475 C.E.)

Bavel: Rabbah Tosfa'ah [Sura], 4228-4234 (468-474 C.E.); Ravina II b. R. Huna [Sura], 4234-4235 (474-475 C.E.), **Termination of Hora'ah.**

Rabbanan Savorai — ca. 4235-4350 (475-590 C.E.).

I.   R. Yose of Pumbedisa, 4236-4276 (476-516 C.E.); R. Achai b. R. Huna. **Close of Babylonian Talmud, 4260 (500 C.E.).**

II. R. Eina [Sura]; R. Simona [Pumb.], 4276-4300 (516-540 C.E.).

III. Ravai of Rov [Pumb.], 4300-4315 (540-555 C.E.).

IV. R. Giza; R. Sama [Peroz Shavor — Pumb.], 4315-4349 (555-589 C.E.). *Redaction of Minor Tractates.*

This Chart is based upon Iggeres RSG, as emended by Rabbi Aharon Hyman. Dates and places rendered represent tenure as Rosh Yeshiva.

For Sources and explanatory notes regarding this Table, see Legacy, Chapters IX, X.

See also Tables XXVIII, XXIX, XXX, for the chronological sequence of the heads of the Academies of Eretz Yisroel, Sura, and Pumbedisa during the Amoraitic period.

Table XXVIII
Eretz Yisroel Roshei Yeshiva - Amoraitic Era

Rosh Yeshiva	Date	Source
Rabbeinu haKadosh (B.S.; Seph.) **Redaction of Mishnah**	d. ca. 190	Legacy, Ch. 8, n. 98
R. Efess (Seph.)	190-215	Legacy, Ch. 9, n. 62
R. Chanina b. Chama (Seph.)	215-240	Legacy, Ch. 9, n. 62
R. Yochanan b. Naphcha (T)— **Laid Foundation of Yerushalmi**	228-288	Legacy, Ch. 9, n. 69
R. Elazar b. Pedas (T)	288	Legacy, Ch. 9, n. 78
R. Ammi (T)	288-305	Legacy, Ch. 9, n. 78
R. Yonah (T)	d. ca. 320	Legacy, Ch. 9, n. 83
R. Yose (T)	d. ca. 325	Legacy, Ch. 9, n. 83
R. Mana b. R. Yonah (Seph.)	d. ca. 352	Legacy, Ch. 9, n. 87
R. Yose b. Bun **Completion of Yerushalmi**	fl. ca. 352	Legacy, Ch. 9, n. 87
Hillel 11—**Calendar Arranged**	359	Legacy, Ch. 9, n. 88

Table XXIX
Roshei Yeshiva of Sura - Amoraitic Era

Rosh Yeshiva	Tenure	IRSG (Hyman)	[Lewin]
Rav (S) **Founded Sura**	219-247	3:2 (65, 68)	[78]
R. Huna (M.M.)	257-297	3:2 (71, n. 43)	[85]
R. Chisda (S)	293-309	3:2 (71, n. 46)	[85]
Rabbah b. R. Huna* (S)	309-320	3:3 (73, n. 7)	[87]
Sura declines	320-352	3:3 (74, n. 17)	[89
R. Papa (Naresh)	352-371	3:3 (74, n. 19)	[89]
R. Ashi (M.M.) **Redaction of Bavli**	371-427	3:4 (81, n. 14)	[94]
Meremar (S)	427-432	3:4 (81, n. 14)	[94]
R. Idi b. Avin 11 (S)	432-452	3:4 (82)	[94]
R. Nachman b. R. Huna (S)	452-455	3:4 (82)	[94]
Mar b. R. Ashi (M.M.)	455-468	3:4 (82)	[951
Rabbah Tosfa'ah (S)	468-474	3:4 (82, n. 16)	[95]
Ravina 11 b. R. Huna (S) **End of Hora'ah**	474-475	3:4 (82, n. 17)	[95]
Sura closed 40 yrs.	475-516	3:4 (82, n. 17)	[97]
R. Eina (S) **First Gaon of Sura**	516-...	3:4 (86)	[99]
R. Mar b. R. Huna (S)	609-620	3:5 (87, n. 3)	[100]

*Rendered lectures, but not officially installed as Rosh Yeshiva.

Table XXX
Roshei Yeshiva of Pumbedisa - Amoraitic Era

Rosh Yeshiva	Tenure	IRSG (Hyman)	[Lewin]
Shmuel (N)	219-254	3:2 (69, n. 28)	[82]
Rabbah b. Avuha (N)*	254-259	3:2 (69, n. 29)	[82]
Nehardea Destroyed	259	3:2 (69, n. 30)	[82]
R. Yehudah b. Yechezkel (P)	257-299	3:2 (71)	[85]
Founded Pumbedisa	257		
Rabbah b. Nachmani (P)	299-320	3:3 (72, n. 3)	[86]
K. Yosef b. Chiyya (P)	320-323	3:3 (73, n. 8)	[87]
Abbaye (P)	326-338	3:3 (73, n. 9)	[87]
Rava (Mechoza)	338-352	3:3 (74)	[89]
R. Nachman b. Yitzchak (P)	352-356	3:3 (75, n. 18)	[89]
R. Chama (N)	356-377	3:3 (76, n. 20)	[89]
R. Zevid (P)	377 -385	3:3 (77)	[90]
R. Dimi of Nehardea (P)	385-388	3:3 (77)	[90]
Rafram b. Papa (P)	388-395	3:3 (77, n. 22)	[90]
R. Kahana IV (P)	395-414	3:3 (77, n. 23)	[90]
Mar Zutra (P)	414-416	3:3 (77, n. 24)	
R. Acha b'rei deRava (P)	416-419	3:3 (77)	[90]
R. Geviha of Bei Kasil (P)	419-433	3:4 (83, n. 18)	[96]
Rafram of Pumbedisa (P)	433-443	3:4 (83, n. 18)	[96]
R. Richomi II (P)	443-456	3:4 (83, n. 20)	[96]
R. Sama b'rei deRava (P)	456-476	3:4 (83, n. 21)	[96]
Rabbanan Savorai		3:4 (86, n. 39)	[97]
R. Yose of Pumbedisa (P)	476-516	3:4 (84, n. 29)	[99]
Completion of Talmud Bavli	500	3:4 (86, n. 39)	[97]
R. Simona (P)	516-540	3:4 (86, n. 39)	[99]
R. Ravai of Rov (P)	540-555	3:4 (86, n. 39)	[99]
Pumb. Closed 30-50 yrs.	555-589	3:5 (86, n. 1)	
Peroz Shavor Founded			
R. Sama; R. Giza (P.S.)	555-589	3:5 (86, n. 1)	
First Gaon of Pumb.			
R. Chanan of Ashkaya (P)	589-608	3:5 (87, n. 2)	[100]

*Rendered lectures, but not officialy installed as Rosh Yeshiva.

Legend: B.S. = Beit She'arim; M.M. = Masa Machsya; M = Mechoza; N = Nehardea
P = Pumbedisa; P.S. = Peroz Shavor; S = Sura; Seph. = Sepphoris; T = Tiberias;
IRSG = Iggeres Rav Sherira Gaon, ( ) = Hyman edition, [ ] = Lewin edition.

THE TEKUFAH OF THE GEONIM

The era of the *Rabbanan Savorai*, which began with the death of Ravina II in 475 C.E., came to a close in 589 C.E., when Mar Chanan of Ashkaya [589-608 C.E.] was installed as the first *Gaon* in the newly reopened Academy of Pumbedisa, after the persecutions had subsided. Twenty years later [609 C.E.], Sura was reopened under Rav Mar bar Rav Huna, as its first *Gaon* [609-620 C.E.].

The *Tekufas haGeonim* lasted 450 years [589-1038 C.E.], when it came to a close with the death of Rav Hai Gaon of Pumbedisa. With but brief interruptions, during the entire Geonic era, the Academies of Sura and Pumbedisa continued to function as the central Torah academies of all Israel, as they had since their establishment at the time of Rav's descent to Bavel more than 800 years earlier, in 219 C.E., at the very outset of the era of the *Amoraim*. Throughout the 800-year history of the Yeshivos, the *Roshei Yeshiva* regarded themselves as the direct spiritual heirs of the Academies of Rav and Shmuel in Sura and Nehardea. For this reason, the row of the most elite scholars in Pumbedisa was known as *Sha'ar Nehardea*.

Among the early *Geonim* was Rav Yehudai Gaon of Sura [751-761 C.E.]. He wrote *Halachos Pesukos*, the earliest extant halachic work of the post-Talmudic period. Rav Yehudai Gaon, who was blind, dictated this work to his *talmidim*.

SHE'ILTOS; BAHAG; ARUCH

The most well-known work of this early period is the *She'iltos* of Rabbeinu Achai miShabcha [ca. 750 C.E.]. It is regarded as a highly authoritative early halachic source.

At about this time, too, Rav Shimon Kayyara wrote his *Halachos Gedolos [BaHaG]*, a halachic work on the *Taryag mitzvos*, which is cited extensively by the *Rishonim*. Rav Zemach b. Paltoi Gaon [Pumbedisa, 871-880] wrote an Aramaic lexicon, the *Aruch*, which clarifies difficult Aramaic terms of the Talmud. Shortly after his tenure, the Yeshivos were moved to Baghdad.

Rav Yosef Gaon [Pumbedisa 815-817] was "exceedingly pious and familiar with miracles." He often had *"Gilui Eliyahu."*

One of the most prolific of all the *Geonim* was Rav Saadiah Gaon [Sura, 928-942 C.E.]. He was in the forefront of the battle against the Karaites. He wrote numerous halachic works, a commentary on *TaNaCh*, and a complete *Seder haTefillos*. His *Emunos veDe'os* is regarded as one of the classic works of Torah philosophy.

THE CLOSING DECADES OF THE GEONIC ERA

As the Geonic era drew to a close towards the latter half of the tenth century, two towering Torah masters emerged, whose eminent spiritual stature was an appropriate epilogue to this glorious era. They were the last *Geonim* of Pumbedisa — Rav Sherira Gaon, and his son, Rav Hai Gaon.

During his forty-year tenure as *Gaon* [968-1006], Rav Sherira Gaon wrote thousands of responsa to Jewish communities all over the world. In response to a question from Rav Yaakov b. Nissim of Kairouan, North Africa, concerning certain aspects of the transmission process, Rav Sherira Gaon wrote his famous *Iggeres Rabbeinu Sherira Gaon*, which provides invaluable information regarding the history of Torah transmission, particularly during the eras of *Tannaim, Amoraim, Rabbanan Savorai,* and *Geonim.*

RAV HAI GAON: END OF A GLORIOUS TEKUFAH

Like his father, during his thirty-five years as *Gaon* of Pumbedisa [1003-1038], three of which overlapped with his father's tenure, Rav Hai Gaon sent thousands of responsa to distant Jewish communities, 1,000 of which have already come to light. Rav Hai Gaon's words are cited frequently by Rabbe Nasan b. Yechiel in his Talmudic lexicon, *haAruch,* by the Rif, the Rambam, the *Ba'alei haTosafos,* and many other *Rishonim.*

Upon the death of Rav Hai Gaon, the Yeshiva of Pumbedisa no longer served as a central Torah Academy. In the same year, the Yeshiva of Sura, too, ceased to function as an independent Torah Academy. The great Academies of Nehardea-Pumbedisa, and Sura-Masa Machsya, which had served as central Torah academies for all Israel for more than eight hundred years, from the descent of Rav to Bavel in 219 C.E. until the death of Rav Hai Gaon in 1038 C.E., no longer served as a central source of Torah guidance for the far-flung Jewish communities all over the world.

Thus it was that with the passing of the last of the great *Geonim,* Rav Hai Gaon, in 1038 C.E. — 2350 years after *Kabbalas haTorah* at Sinai — the last semblance of Torah centralization came to a close, and the *tekufah* of the *Rishonim,* which ushered in an era of Torah dispersal and decentralization, began.

ברוך הנותן ליעף כח, ולאין אונים עצמה ירבה.

ברוך ה' לעולם אמן ואמן. ברוך אתה ה', למדני חקיך. סליק — בס"ד

Table XXXI

THE GEONIC PERIOD
4349-4798 (589-1038 C.E.)

First Century of the Geonic Period: 4349-4449 (589-689 C.E.)

SURA	PEROZ SHAVOR (Nehardea)	PUMBEDISA
Reopened 20 yrs. after Pumbedisa (609 C.E.). (IRSG 3:5, Hyman, n. 3.) R. Mar b. R. Huna* — First Gaon of Sura, 609-620 C.E. R. Chaninai, 620-640 R. Huna, 640-660 (IRSG 3:5, H., n.12) R. Sheshna (R. Mesharsheya b. Tachlifa), 660-670) *R. Sherira Gaon does not render the names of the Geonim of Sura during the ensuing 20 yrs [670-690] (IRSG 3:6, H., n. 16)*	*Established when Sura—Pumb. closed, 30-50 yrs. before Geonic era. Names rendered here are as of beginning of Geonic Era.* R. Mari Sorgo b. R. Dimi, 589-608 C.E., *Transferred to Pumb. (608)* R. Chanina of Bei Gihara, ca. 608-636 R. Yitzchak Gaon, ca. 636-660 *Peroz Shavor combines with Pumbedisa.*	*Geonic era began when Pumb. reopened (589 C.E.) after closing for 30-50 yrs., due to Persian persecution (IRSG 3:5, H., n. 1)* R. Chanan of Ashkaya* — First Gaon, 589-608 C.E. R. Mari Sorgo b. R. Dimi, 608-620 C.E., *Ancestor of R. Sherira Gaon* R. Chana Gaon, ca. 620-640 R. Rava, 640-660 (IRSG 3:5, H., n. 12) R. Bustenai, ca. 660-689 R. Hana Mari b. R. Yosef, ca. 689

Second Century of the Geonic Period: 4449-4556 (689-796)

SURA	PUMBEDISA
Mar R. Chanina of Nehar Pekod, 689-694 C.E. (IRSG 3:6) Mar R. Nehilai haLevi of Naresh, 694-712 Mar R. Yaakov haKohen of Nehar Pekod, 712-730 Mar R. Shmuel (descendant of the Amora, Ameimar, and grandson of R. Rava Gaon of Pumb.), 730-748 Mar R. Mari haKohen of Nehar Pekod, 748-756 Mar R. Acha (originally from Pumb.), 756 R. Yehudai Gaon (b. Nachman),* 757-761, *Halachos Pesukos (Hilchos Re'u). His halachic decisions are cited extensively by the Rishonim* Mar R. Achunai Kahana b. Mar Papa, 761-768 (IRSG 3:6; H., n. 25) Mar R. Chanina Kahana b. R. Huna, 768-776 Mar R. Mari haLevi b. Mar R. Mesharsheya, 776-780 [R. Shimon Kayyara,* *Halachos Gedolos (Bahag), cited extensively by the Rishonim*] Mar R. Bibai haLevi b. Mar R. Rava of Nehar Pekod, 780-790, *Joined Geonei Pumbedisa to enact takanah of Geviyas Metaltelin — debt collection from movable property.*	Mar R. Chiyya of Meshan Mar R. Ravya (or Mar R. Abbaye) Mar R. Natronai b. Mar R. Nechemiah, ca. 719 C.E. R. Yehudah R. Yosef (or Mar Kusnai), 739-748 R. Shmuel b. Mar R. Mari, 748-755 [R. Achai of Shabcha,* ca. 680-760, *She'iltos, cited extensively by the Rishonim*] R. Natroi Kahana b. Mar R. Amunah, 755-759 R. Avraham Kahana, 759-761 R. Dodai b. R. Nachman (brother of R. Yehudai Gaon of Sura), 761-764 R. Chanina b. R. Mesharsheya, 764-771 R. Malcha b. Mar Acha, 771-773 Mar R. Rava b. R. Dodai (ancestor of RSG, 773-782) R. Shinoi, ca. 782 R. Chanina Kahana b. R. Avraham Gaon, 783-786 Mar R. Huna haLevi b. Yitzchak, 786-788, *Enacted Takanas Metaltelin* R. Menasheh b. R. Yosef, 788-796, *Enacted Takanas Metaltelin*

Table XXXI (cont'd)

Third Century of the Geonic Period: 4550-4651 (790-891 C.E.)

SURA

Mar R. Hilai bar Mar R. Mari, 790-798 C.E.

R. Yaakov haKohen b. Mar R. Mordecai, 798-812

R. Avomai (uncle of R. Yaakov Gaon), 813-821

Mar R. Zadok b. R. Ashi, 821-823

R. Hilai b. Mar R. Chanina, 823-827

Mar R. Kiyomi bar Mar R. Ashi, 827-830

R. Moshe (or Mesharsheya) b. Mar R. Yaakov Kahana, 830-841

No Gaon in Sura for 2 yrs., 841-843

R. Kohen Zedek b. Mar R. Avomai Gaon, 843-848

R. Sar Shalom b. Boaz, 848-853

R. Natronai b. R. Hilai Gaon, 853-858

R. Amram Gaon (b. Sheshna),* 858-876, *Siddur Rav Amram Gaon (Seder haTefillos)*

R. Nachshon b. Mar R. Zadok, 876-884

R. Zemach b. Mar Chaim, 884-891

Mar R. Malcha, 891 C.E.

PUMBEDISA

Mar R. Yeshayah haLevi b. Mar Abba, 796-798 C.E.

Mar R. Yosef b. Mar R. Shila of Shalchi, 798-805

Mar R. Kahana b. R. Chanina b. R. Avraham, 805-811

Mar R. Ivomai b. Mar R. Avraham Gaon, 811-815

Mar R. Yosef b. Abba,* 815-817, *Had Gilui Eliyahua*

Mar R. Avraham b. Mar R. Sherira, 817-828

R. Yosef b. Mar Chiyya, 828-833

Mar R. Yitzchak b. Mar R. Chanina, 833-838

Mar R. Yosef b. Mar R. Rivai, 839-841

R. Paltoi b. Mar Abbaye, 841-857, *Wrote Commentary on Talmud; Extensive Responsa.*

R. Achai b. Mar Rav, 857

R. Menachem b. Mar R. Yosef b. Chiyya, 857-859

R. Mattisyah b. R. Ravi, 859-868

R. Abba b. Ammi (grandson of R. Shmuel Gaon), 869-870

R. Zemach b. R. Paltoi Gaon,* 871-880, *Aruch (Talmudic lexicon)*

R. Hai b. R. David — 1st Gaon in Baghdad, 880-888

Fourth Century of the Geonic Period: 4648-4798 (888-1038 C.E.)

SURA

Mar R. Hai b. R. Nachshon Gaon, 892-898

Mar R. Hilai b. Natronai, 898-905

Mar R. Shalom b. R. Mishael, 905-911

R. Yaakov b. Natronai, 911-923

R. Yom Tov Kahana b. Mar R. Yaakov, 923-927

R. Saadiah Gaon (b. Yosef),* 928-942, *Emunos veDeos, Siddur, et. al., Prolific author, fought Karaites.*

R. Yosef b. Yaakov, 942-944

Academy of Sura closed for 45 years

R. Zemach b. Yitzchak, 988-997

R. Shmuel b. Chofni* (father-in-law of R. Hai Gaon), 997-1013, *Wrote many Sefarim (not extant)*

R. Dosa b. R. Saadiah Gaon, 1013-1017

R. Yisroel b. R. Shmuel b. Chofni, 1017-1034

R. Azariah haKohen (b. Rav Yisroel?), 1034-1038

R. Yitzchak — last Gaon of Sura, 1038-...

The Yeshivos remained open, first independently, and then as a united Yeshiva in Baghdad for 150 years longer, but they no longer served as central Torah academies for the entire Golah.

PUMBEDISA

Mar R. Kiyomi b. Mar R. Achai Gaon, 888-906 C.E.

R. Yehudah b. R. Shmuel (grandfather of R. Sherira Gaon), 906-917

R. Mevasser Kahana b. Mar Kiyomi Gaon, 917-926

Mar R. Kohen Zedek Kahana b. Mar R. Yosef, 926-935

R. Zemach b. R. Kafnai, 935-938

R. Chanina b. Yehudah Gaon (father of R. Sherira Gaon), 938-944

R. Aharon b. Mar R. Yosef haKohen, 944-960

R. Nechemiah b. Mar R. Kohen Zedek, 960-968

R. Sherira Gaon (b. R. Chanina Gaon),* 968-1006, *Extensive Responsa; Iggeres R. Sherira Gaon, dated 986*

[Arba'ah Shevuyyim (Four Captive Scholars), ca. 995]

R. Hai Gaon (b. R. Sherira Gaon),* 1003-1038, *Halachic codes, e.g. Mekach u-Memkar, Sha'arei Shevu'os; Extensive Responsa; Cited extensively by the Rishonim; Disciples worldwide; Last major Gaon.*

Close of Geonic Era

This Chart is based upon Iggeres RSG (Hyman edition) and upon Doros haRishonim of Rav Yitzchak Isaac haLevi, Vol. IV — Tekufas haGeonim; Supplemented by Tekufas haGeonim veSafrusah, of Rabbi Simcha Assaf, pp. 51, 53, 125.

*Geonim with an asterisk after their names are discussed more fully in Legacy of Sinai.

Table XXXII
Primary Dates in Jewish History

Date	Significant Events	Source
1	**Creation**	Gen. 1:1
1656	Mabbul	Gen. 7:6
1948	Birth of Avraham	Gen. 11:26
2048	Birth of Yitzchak	Gen. 21:5
2108	Birth of Yaakov	Gen. 25:26
2368	Birth of Moshe	Ex. 2:1,R
2448	**Exodus—Revelation**	Ex. 12:40,R
2488	Entered Eretz Yisroel	Josh. 4:19
2516	Era of Zekenim—Shoftim	Judg. 3:11
2871	Era of Nvi'im	Appen. B, n. 13
2928	**Construction of 1st Temple**	1 K 6:1
2964	Secession of Ten Tribes	1 K 11:31; 12:16
3205	Exile of Ten Tribes	II K 18:9-10
3338	**Destruction of 1st Temple**	II K 25:8-9; Yoma 9a
ca. 3370	Era of Anshei Knesses haGedolah	Legacy, Ch. 6, n. 71
3405	Miracle of Purim	S.O. 29
3408	**Construction of 2nd Temple**	Chag. 1:1-14
3448	Termination of Prophecy	Legacy, Ch. 5, n. 1
ca. 3500	Era of Zugos	Legacy, Ch. 7, n. 30
3622	Miracle of Chanukah	Avod. Zar. 9a
ca. 3728	Seven Middos of Hillel	Legacy, Ch. 7, n. 78
ca. 3768	Era of Tannaim	Legacy, Ch. 7, n. 80
	Targum Yonasan b. Uziel	Legacy, Ch. 8, n. 7
3828	**Destruction of 2nd Temple**	Yoma 9a
ca. 3870	Two Mechiltos	Legacy, Ch. 8, n. 76
ca. 3890	Targum Onkelos	Legacy, Ch. 8, n. 78
3948	**Redaction of Mishnah**	Legacy, Ch. 8, n. 98
3950	Era of Amoraim	Legacy, Ch. 9, n. 41
3960	Tosefta, Baraisos Redacted	Legacy, Ch. 9, n. 15
3970	Sifra, Sifrei Redacted	Legacy, Ch. 9, n. 52
3979	Rav Settles in Bavel	Legacy, Ch. 9, n. 29
4112	**Completion of Talmud Yerushalmi**	Legacy, Ch. 9, n. 87
4119	Permanent Calender	Legacy, Ch. 9, n. 88
4235	Termination of Hora'ah	Legacy, Ch. 10, n. 152
4235	Era of Rabbanan Savorai	Legacy, Ch. 11, n. 17
4260	**Completion of Talmud Bavli**	Legacy, Ch. 11, n. 18
4349	Geonic Era	Legacy, Ch. 11, n. 25
ca. 4510	Halachos Pesukos	Legacy, Ch. 11, n. 43
ca. 4510	She'iltos	Legacy, Ch. 11, n. 50
ca. 4540	BaHaG	Legacy, Ch. 11, n. 55
4798	**End of Geonic Era**	Legacy, Ch. 12, n. 9

Appen.—Appendix; Avod. Zar.—Avodah Zarah; Chag.—Chagigah;
Ch. — Chapter; Ex. — Exodus; Gen. — Genesis; Josh. — Joshua;
Judg.—Judges; K—Kings; n.—note; R—Rashi; S.O.—Seder Olam.

Table XXXIII

Daniel's Vision Concerning the Four Kingdoms
(See Legacy of Sinai, p. 129, n. 1)

In the Book of Daniel (Chaps. 2 and 7), and in the prophecies of Zechariah b. Berechiah (Chap. 6), we are apprised of a vision concerning Four Kingdoms which would rule the earth in direct succession, beginning with the era of the First Churban. The Four Kingdoms, which are symbolized by Daniel as four terrifying beasts, and by Zechariah as four horse-drawn chariots, represented the kingdoms of Babylon, Persia, Greece, and Rome. (See Avodah Zarah 2b.) According to the the Ibn Ezra (Daniel 7:14), the fourth kingdom refers to the Arab Kingdom, while Rome is included with the Greeks in the third kingdom. The Ramban, however, refutes this view entirely, and maintains that the fourth kingdom refers to "wicked" Rome, following the Talmud in Avodah Zarah 2b and elsewhere. (See Sefer haGeulah, Kisvei Ramban, Chavel ed. [Jerusalem: Mosad haRav Kook, 1963], Vol. I, Sha'ar 3, p. 284. See also Ramban, Numbers 24:20, Chavel ed. [Mosad haRav Kook, 1963]). The following is a chronological outline of these four kingdoms, according to Seder Olam, Ch. 28 (G'ra, n. 7), and Ch. 30, as well as Avodah Zarah 2b, 8b, and 9a.

Dates	Legacy Pages	Dynasty and Primary Events
I. Babylon *(Galus Bavel — in present-day Iraq)*		
3319-3364	109-110	Nebuchadnezzar
3320	109; 186	*Judah comes under Babylonian rule*
3327	109; 187	*Galus Yehoiakim; Galus Yehoiachin*
3338	104-106	***First Temple Destroyed***
3364-3386	110	Evil-Merodach
3364	110	*Yehoiachin released from dungeon*
3386-3389	110, n. 14	Belshazzar
3389	110	*Handwriting on the Wall*
II. Persia-Media *(Paras u'Maddai — in present-day Iran)*		
3389-3390	111	Darius I, the Mede
3390-3392	111; 119	Cyrus the Persian
3390	111; 120	*Grants permission to rebuild Temple*
3393	121, n. 76	Artaxerxes (Cambyses)
3393	120, n. 74	*Rescinds permission to rebuild Temple*
3393-3407	121	Ahasuerus
3395-3405	121	***Story of Purim***
3407-3442	113; 121	Darius II, the Persian*
3408	113; 121	***Completion of Temple authorized***
		*(Deposed — 3442; Slain — 3448)
III. Greece *(Yavan)*		
3442-3454	114; 125	Alexander the Great
3442/3448	79; 123	***Termination of Prophecy***
3449	125, n. 97	*Minyan Shetaros begins*
3454-3622	129; 137	Ptolemaic [Egypt] and Seleucid [Syrian] Dynasties
3515	136	*Ptolemy Philadelphus — Septuagint*
3562	137	*Seleucids wrest control of Judea from Ptolemies*
3622	138	***Chashmonean uprising — Story of Chanukah***
IV. Rome *(Galus Edom)*		
3622	139	*Initial conquest of Greece*
3648	139	*Rome reneges on alliance with Chashmonaim*
3697	140	*Pompey captures Jerusalem during Jewish civil war*
3712	48 B.C.E.	*Julius Caesar confirms Jewish privileges*
3730	30 B.C.E.	*Augustus Caesar [Octavian] establishes and consolidates Roman Empire*